PENGU

HEALTHY TRAD
FOR YOUR

Beverley Piper is a qualified home economist and cookery teacher. She lives in Ashford, Kent, where she writes her books and magazine articles and teaches microwave cookery from her own test kitchen as well as giving public demonstrations to large audiences around the country. She has appeared regularly on BBC television's *Pebble Mill at One* demonstrating microwave cooking, and also broadcasts on radio. Her other publications include *Microwave Cooking*, *Cooking in Colour – Microwave Cooking*, *Microwaving for Ones and Twos* and *Microwave Cooking for Health* (Penguin 1987).

Beverley Piper has two teenage sons.

HEALTHY TRADITIONAL RECIPES FOR YOUR MICROWAVE

Beverley Piper

PENGUIN BOOKS

PENGUIN BOOKS

Published by the Penguin Group
27 Wrights Lane, London W8 5TZ, England
Viking Penguin Inc., 40 West 23rd Street, New York, New York 10010, USA
Penguin Books Australia Ltd, Ringwood, Victoria, Australia
Penguin Books Canada Ltd, 2801 John Street, Markham, Ontario, Canada L3R 1B4
Penguin Books (NZ) Ltd, 182–190 Wairau Road, Auckland 10, New Zealand

Penguin Books Ltd, Registered Offices: Harmondsworth, Middlesex, England

First published 1989
1 3 5 7 9 10 8 6 4 2

Printed and bound in Great Britain by
Cox & Wyman Ltd, Reading
Filmset in Century Schoolbook (Linotron 202) by
Rowland Phototypesetting Ltd,
Bury St Edmunds, Suffolk

For Anne and Chris, Roe and Rodger,
without whose constant support this book
might never have been finished!

CONTENTS

A Little History

Rudimentary ovens are thought to have existed even in the primitive world, but cooking facilities in the houses of ordinary people remained quite basic until as late as the nineteenth century. Royalty and nobility, of course, had large kitchens, in which food was mostly cooked over an open flame, in large pots or on a spit, or in makeshift clay ovens. The lower classes cooked either over the fire that also heated their house or hut, or outdoors. Bread was baked in a clay pot by covering it with hot ashes. Royal courts and monasteries often solved the problem of feeding their large numbers by taking advantage of the law that compelled commoners to provide meat, fish, cheese, bread and other fresh food sufficient to feed the local monastery, manor house, or the king's retinue as it travelled around the country.

It is difficult today for us to imagine a kitchen without the labour-saving equipment we have come not simply to accept but to expect as our right. Imagine having to start the day washing clothes in a stream, getting them clean by using a washing-stone, then taking the harvested corn to be ground at the mill before being able to make the bread that was such an important part of the whole family's diet. However, for all their shortcomings, people in medieval England probably had a more healthy diet than we do today, for they ate bread, thick soups, dishes made from milk, eggs, butter, peas and, of course, fruit from the hedgerows as well as apples and pears. Meat was available to the poor only if the family were able to keep a pig, or hunt for hare or rabbit, but as poaching laws existed, they risked the loss of a limb if caught, so meat did not often form part of the diet.

Salt was obviously very important, as it was about the only form of food preservation available. It was used to salt down any meat that could be saved for winter use.

By the early nineteenth century things had improved considerably in England. A different class structure began to emerge, and the more wealthy tradesmen, professionals and owners of large households began to require houses that had kitchens set apart from their own quarters but which were still controlled by them.

It was often the mistress of the house who supervised the menu and the kitchen staff and who was the overseer of the kitchen garden, where herbs and vegetables were grown in profusion. These were then made into imaginative dishes for the master and mistress by the head cook and her kitchen-maids. Work was hard and hours long, but the staff were basically content to have somewhere to live and were pleased to accept a very small wage, as their meals and lodgings were provided free.

As we use our fan-assisted ovens, microwave ovens, food processors, electric mixers, washing-machines and dish-washers, we should remember that it was not until the middle of the nineteenth century that the first closed-in cooking range evolved. It was heated by coal and had a flue, which took the fumes to the chimney. Imagine having the job of lighting the range every morning! This task fell to the youngest kitchen-maid, who often had to rise before dawn so that she had time to clean out the fire and relight it before continuing with her other duties.

Other labour-saving devices followed on quite quickly after the invention of the range – kitchen scales, Dutch ovens, meat presses and mincers all made life for the kitchen staff a little easier. The kitchens themselves were highly organized and generally kept scrupulously clean. They needed to be, for often eleven or twelve people worked under the cook in one capacity or another, so a badly planned, unorganized kitchen would have spelled disaster.

The large pine or deal tables for which one would pay considerable amounts of money at auctions today were used extensively both for food preparation and as dining-tables for the staff, and later, if time allowed, card games and dice were played on them for recreation. Pine dressers, also, are now very fashionable in our kitchens and dining-rooms. They were and still are used to store crockery and cutlery. Both these basics of kitchen furniture were frequently scrubbed down by the kitchen-maids to ensure they were scrupulously clean.

Refrigerators and freezers were not available in the nineteenth century, and although English fruits and vegetables were cheap and plentiful they were obviously seasonal, so it fell to the cook to devise ways of preserving summer gluts for winter use. Jams, jellies, marmalade, chutneys and pickles were all made in the preserving pans owned by every household. Towards the end of the nineteenth century, food manufacturers produced bottled and tinned foods, but many cooks continued to make their own, buying fresh produce from the vast markets where almost all the foodstuffs were purchased. They preferred the flavour of 'home-made', and having been brought up in an environment where the sugar was cut from great blocks and all the spices ground by hand before the fruits and vegetables were prepared and cooked, they would probably have felt cheated if the vast task of preservation were removed from them and the finished product could instead be bought straight from the corner shop, along with the flour, salt and lentils!

TRADITIONAL RECIPES MADE HEALTHY

Traditional cookery brings to mind those wonderful highly calorific recipes that have become part of our heritage – steak and kidney pie and pudding, bacon and onion roly-poly, toad in the hole, rice pudding, Sussex pond pudding, apple pie, trifle and plum duff to name but a few. After searching through old cookery and history books, I used traditional recipes to trigger off ideas for the recipes found on the following pages.

In keeping with the sensible and necessary vogue for healthy eating, this book is designed for those who wish to continue to enjoy traditional fare but who would prefer to use recipes with healthy foodstuffs in their lists of ingredients.

The following recipes have been compiled to have wide appeal, to be visually attractive, to be not too high in calories and to use good quality ingredients that are readily available. Many adapt traditional recipes, cutting the fat content, replacing some of the sugar with dried fruit and substituting yoghurt for cream. Full-fat milk is replaced by semi-skimmed milk, or stock in the savoury dishes, while white flour is replaced partly or wholly by healthier wholemeal. Hopefully many of the changes will go undetected, and yet by following the recipes you will quickly be adapting to a healthier lifestyle.

All the recipes are designed to be cooked in a microwave oven – one of the most exciting modern kitchen appliances to have been developed during our time. In addition there is a special section of recipes for combination ovens, which combine microwave and hot-air cooking.

NUTRITION

A basic knowledge of nutrition is necessary so that we understand why old-fashioned eating habits are no longer considered to be healthy. Simply take the traditional 'farmhouse' breakfast – fried bacon, eggs and sausage with fried bread, mushrooms and tomatoes, followed by toast and marmalade, all swilled down with plenty of sweet tea!

It is now widely recognized that frying is the most unhealthy method of cooking. One gram of calorie-laden fat contains 9 calories, while 1 gram of either protein or carbohydrate contains only 4 calories. Animal fats have been closely associated with heart disease and obesity, as they clog arteries and, when not burnt by the body to provide energy, lay down deposits of fat, which we all know are extremely difficult to shift! It therefore becomes abundantly clear why this 'farmhouse' breakfast is bad news indeed. A far healthier alternative would be baked beans on wholemeal toast spread with one of the low-fat spreads, or a bowl of wholesome homemade muesli, made using dried fruits as sweeteners instead of sugar, and served with semi-skimmed milk or yoghurt.

Fat is necessary in our diets as it is a wonderful source of energy and is needed to cushion the organs in our bodies. However, fat is found in varying amounts in almost every food we eat so it is highly unlikely that we would be deprived in any way if we cut down our consumption of fat; indeed we would almost certainly benefit.

Cholesterol is the type of fat that ends up in the walls of our arteries, causing heart problems, particularly in the middle and later years. Cholesterol is viewed as the 'enemy' as it is closely linked with heart disease. It is necessary, but, as the human body itself produces all the cholesterol it needs, it is dangerous to take in a lot more by eating foods that are high in cholesterol.

The Americans are far more aware of and, therefore, wary of cholesterol than we are, and we should learn more about high-cholesterol food, which is best avoided. Polyunsaturated fats such as vegetable margarines should be used whenever possible in place of animal fats such as butter and animal-fat margarines, which are high in cholesterol.

Vegetable oils are other polyunsaturated alternatives, but remember that the calorific value of all cooking oils is higher than that of butter, lard or margarine.

Cholesterol is also high in egg yolks, liver and kidneys, and these should be eaten in moderation.

BALANCING FOODS

Carbohydrates, fats, proteins, vitamins, minerals and fibre – these are the accepted categories into which all the foods we eat are divided. We have already discussed **fats**, which are sometimes used to provide energy. **Carbohydrates** are the main energy-giving foods. The body uses carbohydrate foods, such as bread, rice and potatoes, to give us energy, leaving the **protein** foods, e.g. milk, cheese, meat, fish, eggs and pulses, to perform their role of replacing worn body tissue or, in the case of children, of building new body tissue, which perhaps explains why the protein foods are so important.

Vitamins and minerals are vital in very small quantities to enable the body to function normally. They are present in many foods, and anyone eating a reasonably varied diet should not have to take supplements.

EXAMPLES OF VITAMINS

Vitamin A, commonly known as the anti-infection vitamin, is necessary to prevent infection attacking the body; it is also needed for good eyesight. It is chiefly found in ox liver, fish-liver oils, green leafy vegetables, carrots, cheese, milk, butter and margarine. **Vitamin D** is necessary for healthy bones and teeth. It is concentrated in fish-liver oils, butter, egg yolks, margarine and liver. It is also produced in the skin due to the effect of ultra-violet rays in sunshine. **Calcium**, a mineral found in significant quantities in milk and milk products (particularly Cheddar cheese), white bread, dried fruit and green vegetables, and in small quantities in white fish and eggs, is also necessary for healthy bones and teeth.

DIETARY FIBRE

Dietary fibre comes from plant foods. All cereals, fruit and vegetables have some fibre, but certain foods have more fibre than others. Basically fibre is the indigestible carbohydrate found in plant foods. Up until the advent of the F-plan diet in

1982 it was known as roughage! Its important property as far as dieting is concerned is that it cannot be digested by man. So although fibre is wonderful at making us feel full, as it is not absorbed but is instead expelled by the bowel, it cannot be turned into body fat. Therefore, a diet that is high in fibre and low in fat and digestible carbohydrate usually means weight loss without hunger pangs. Care must be taken, however, to ensure that sufficient protein is included in the diet. Also, too much fibre will impede the absorption of certain minerals.

THE FIGHT AGAINST SUGAR

Consumption of sugar starts as a habit. As children many of us were given a sweet or a biscuit or a sweetened drink in a bottle as a pacifier. Sugar does provide energy but it has very little food value, and the body readily produces its own sugar from complex carbohydrate foods like bread.

Try cutting the amount of sugar by half in cake recipes and use no sugar at all when dried fruits are used – you will hardly notice its absence. Sugar causes tooth decay, and it is also high in calories, so will quickly add the pounds. Rather like giving up sugar in tea and coffee, once those agonizing first couple of weeks have passed you'll probably prefer to cook most of your food without sugar and will never return to the sugar habit again!

A HEALTHY DIET

To establish a healthy diet we should aim to use a wide variety of foods in balanced proportions. Try to make more use of fresh fruit, salad ingredients and fresh vegetables. Experiment with pulses, nuts and rice and use them to extend the protein foods. In so doing you will naturally start to cut down on red meat and dairy products, which are high in fat, because you will be feeling full from the 'healthy' foods.

Fish is a particularly valuable food, but one which is still vastly under-used in this country. It is high in protein, calcium and other minerals, and white fish has only traces of fat in its flesh while oily fish has polyunsaturated fat (the healthier type of fat) distributed throughout its tissue. These oily fish, e.g. mackerel, trout and sardines, are, therefore, a good source of fat-soluble vitamins A and D and an excellent alternative to red meat, which is high in saturated fat.

Foods with high fat contents have high calorie counts – compare the calorie count of 28g (1 oz) of cod, which is 22 calories, with the calorie count of Cheddar cheese – 28g (1 oz) contains 115 calories. It becomes very clear which of the two foods harbours a high fat content. It also shows how sensible it is to serve dishes that use small amounts of high-calorie foods, eked out with high-fibre foods such as vegetables and pulses.

The recipes in this book aim to do just that. You may notice that when you follow them your shopping list will comprise less red meat but more vegetables, grains, fish, low-fat cheeses, etc. This will probably also help your pocket a little. You will find that modern ingredients such as *fromage frais*, reduced-fat curd cheese, semi-skimmed milk and low-fat dairy spreads are used where possible to lighten the calorie count of a recipe without drastically changing the taste or appearance of the finished dish.

One interesting point I discovered during my research was that tomatoes were once grown primarily for their attractive appearance, but they were regarded with much suspicion, probably due to their bright colour, and were not used in cooking until quite recently. They are now valued for their colour, flavour and vitamin content, and I have used plenty of both fresh and canned tomatoes in the recipes.

A WORD ABOUT MILK

Recently much confusion has arisen about milk, and many people are avoiding it, as it has received some adverse publicity. However, it is a valuable food that is available on our doorsteps every morning. This extremely cheap, high-protein dairy product is very versatile and can be used in sweet and savoury dishes alike as well as being served simply as a drink or on cereals. Milk is high in calcium, which is vitally necessary throughout our lives. Skimmed or semi-skimmed milk should be used where possible, as half the fat has been removed from semi-skimmed and almost all the fat has been removed from skimmed. Children, unless on a diet to reduce fats for some reason, benefit from the energy-giving value of whole milk. Skimmed and semi-skimmed milk have the same, or higher, calcium, protein and vitamin content as whole milk, but with fewer calories.

USING A MICROWAVE OVEN

HOW DOES A MICROWAVE WORK?

Microwave cooking is quick, clean and economical, but how does an oven that doesn't get hot itself cook our food? The answer is very simple: the microwave cooks by friction heat.

The domestic microwave oven plugs into a normal 13-amp socket, and it is the MAGNETRON in the microwave that converts normal electricity into microwave energy. This energy is transmitted into the microwave oven cavity where it bounces off the metal interior and acts on the molecules in the food, causing them to vibrate at a speed that is faster than the speed of light – therefore, it is impossible for the naked human eye to detect what is going on. This terrific vibration occurs in the outermost 1″ to 1½″ of the food. It causes friction heat, which is passed to the centre of the food by conduction and the food is cooked. The energy is shared between whatever food is placed in the microwave, so it must be remembered that the more you increase the load, the longer it will take to cook: e.g. 450 g (1 lb) potatoes will take 9 minutes to cook in a 700W oven but 900 g (2 lb) will take about 12–13 minutes. A standing or resting time is also important. The food continues to cook once the food has been removed from the oven. Cover the food, which will help to keep the heat in, and set it aside on the work top while it 'stands'. This method means that you may continue to use the microwave for another recipe, while the cooking process is being completed.

Do remember that cooking containers will also become hot in the microwave, so when handling them, always use oven gloves.

TYPES OF MICROWAVE OVEN AVAILABLE

As a prospective purchaser with little or no former knowledge, to walk into a large electrical store with the view of selecting a microwave oven must be mind-boggling. There are now a large number of models on the market, all at vastly different prices, and many seem to have something special to attract the undiscerning buyer to that particular model.

In my opinion it is vital to do a little research and gain some knowledge of microwave ovens before being confronted with this situation.

TIPS FOR THE WOULD-BE PURCHASER

1. Read at least two microwave cookery books. Look at the pictures and decide whether you actually wish to cook with a microwave or whether you are going to use it just as a re-heater and defroster.

2. Attend demonstrations or a course of evening classes so that you know a) the speed and method of cooking, b) what the finished food looks like and c) what the food tastes like.

3. Understand WATTAGE, or OUTPUT, and realize that the higher the wattage, the quicker the microwave will cook or re-heat your food. Do you need terrific speed?

4. Consider the size and location of the oven in your kitchen. Find out if it is top- or rear-vented, as the air must be allowed to circulate and a small gap is necessary above or behind the vent.

5. Consider whether it is possible to build the oven in, if this would suit your kitchen layout.

6. Do you want a turntable? This is personal preference, as now most models cook fairly evenly using either a turntable, which turns the food through the microwave energy, or the other method, a stirrer fan in the top or base of the oven, which circulates the energy while the food remains static. With both methods, **stirring or turning food is still important and a necessary part of microwave cooking**. Remember, also, that the turntable is sometimes breakable and expensive to replace.

7. Would you like a touch-pad microprocessor oven? If so, will all members of the family be able to use it successfully?

8. Cost – don't pay for a sophisticated microprocessor oven with memory, automatic cooking, meat probe, browner, etc. if you are not going to use the sophistication to its full advantage.

9. Browning dish – don't be talked into buying a browning dish at the same time as purchasing your microwave oven. If you decide you would like one, you can always go back, and you may find that, as the browning dish needs pre-heating before use, it is preferable to brown the food under your conventional grill after microwaving.

COMBINATION OVENS

The popularity of these microwaves, which brown and microwave at the same time, is ever increasing. In simple lay-language, most of them combine a fan-assisted oven with microwave energy, which work simultaneously. Combination models may also be used just as microwave ovens or just as fan-assisted ovens, and often there is a grill, which may be used on its own or in conjunction with microwave power. As a lot of the cooking on these models can be done using an automatic setting, I suggest that new owners take pains to ensure that they use their model to its full advantage and that they also learn to use it as a microwave alone. Combination ovens are useful for couples living alone who may wish to replace their conventional ovens.

WATTAGE

The output of the oven, or the speed at which it cooks, is described in watts. The most powerful domestic microwaves available are 700W, and the least powerful are 450W. A 700W oven will cook food considerably quicker than its 450W counterpart. It is normally the ovens of 650W and 700W that may have technical optional extras such as automatic defrost, autosensor cooking, meat probes and browning facilities.

'Automatic weight defrost' means that by simply pressing touch-pads (to enter the weight of the food) and selecting DEFROST, the microwave will calculate how long the particular piece of frozen food will take to defrost.

An autosensor works out the cooking time of many dishes by judging the amount of steam being released. The steam is detected by the humidity sensor and the oven automatically calculates the remaining cooking time.

A meat probe is inserted into the centre of a joint and registers the internal temperature of the meat in a viewing panel, so you know at a glance when to take the joint out of the oven and let it stand. They are also useful when re-heating such dishes as casseroles and lasagne.

The prices of microwaves vary considerably with their sophistication, so do make quite sure that you have chosen an oven that will suit your individual needs.

VERSATILITY

The microwave is a marvellous piece of kitchen equipment which is extremely versatile. It is much more than just a defroster and re-heater. Use the microwave for all these cooking methods and you will begin to see the value of the magical box on your kitchen work-top.

1. **Boiling.** The microwave will cook rice to separate-grain perfection and cooks pasta perfectly. Vegetables can be cooked in very little water, preserving colour, nutrients and flavour. Pulses cook in far less time and with less trouble than when they are cooked conventionally.

2. **Steaming.** For invalids, or just for healthy eating, steam fish and vegetables, fruits and puddings.

3. **Simmering.** Use the 40%/SIMMER or 30%/DEFROST setting on the variable power facility on your microwave for milk puddings, pulses, casseroles, custards and rich fruit cakes.

4. **Frying.** Shallow-fat frying with the minimum of oil is easy using a pre-heated browning dish. Fish cakes, croquettes and the like are all very successful. *Don't* attempt to deep-fat fry, as it is not possible to control the temperature of the oil sufficiently.

5. **Poaching.** Eggs can be poached perfectly. Try fruits poached in fruit juice and fish poached in stock or semi-skimmed milk.

6. **Sauces.** All kinds of sauces, sweet and savoury, are quick, easy and successful. There is very little washing-up afterwards, too, as usually only one container is needed, and microwave cooking doesn't bake the food on to the container.

7. **Roasting.** All types of meat, poultry and game roast well, and joints of 1.4 kg (3 lb) and over will colour quite successfully. Always place the joint in a roasting bag on a microwave roasting rack so that the joint cooks and the fat runs away!

8. **Softening.** Ingredients such as onions and celery may be quickly softened before being added to a casserole or similar dish – far healthier than conventional frying in fat. Butter or margarine may be softened dramatically quickly for spreading or for creaming.

9. **Baking.** Cakes and biscuits cook quickly with excellent results – see recipes in the baking section.

10. **Melting.** Chocolate may be melted on the 40%/SIMMER control without fiddling around with bowls of hot water! It tends to melt in its shape, so remember to stir frequently and remove when almost melted. Gelatine is also very easy to deal with in the microwave.

11. **Preserving.** Jams, chutneys and curds are full of flavour and colour when made the microwave way. Far less trouble to cook, too.

12. **Sweet-making.** Rum truffles, coconut ice, toffee and fudge are all popular traditional sweets, which can be made in the microwave with little fuss, but are definitely not recommended for those following a healthy eating campaign.

13. **Stewing and casseroling.** Whole joints may be braised on a bed of vegetables and meat, and microwaved vegetable stews are full of flavour and very tender.

DISHES TO USE IN THE MICROWAVE

There are many special dishes now available for microwave cookery. These can be useful, as they have been specifically designed for the job for which they are intended. However, remember that you will have plenty of containers in your kitchen that you will be able to use in the microwave. Pyrex, high-grade plastics, pottery, china and ceramics are all useful. Containers made partly or wholly of metal, however, should not be used, as they will deflect the microwave rays, preventing the food from cooking, and possibly damaging the oven. This includes dishes with metal trim or handles. Similarly, tin foil should not generally be used in a microwave. Small pieces, however, can be used to mask, for example, chicken wings, which may overcook if left uncovered. Check in the manual supplied with your oven to see whether tin foil can be used in your particular model. Do be careful to choose a dish that is as similar as possible to the one described in the recipe. Many people do not realize that using the wrong dish can mean disastrous results!

WHY USE THE MICROWAVE TO COOK TRADITIONAL RECIPES?

a *Speed*

Many old-fashioned recipes such as rice pudding, Christmas pudding, steak and kidney pudding, etc. take a long, long time to cook conventionally. Today we lead very busy lives, more often than not combining a full-time job with cooking for the family. The microwave is able to cook these recipes in one third to one quarter of the time it would take to cook them conventionally, with a saving of fuel and time. The microwave oven is also cheap to run, costing about 6p for a full hour's use.

b *Cleanliness*
There is probably no cleaner method of cooking. The microwave interior never gets really hot, as the heat is contained within the food, so cleaning is simply a quick wipe over with a dishcloth. The cooking containers are also far easier to wash up as microwave food doesn't 'bake on'.

c *Table-top height*
As the microwave fits on a work-top, there is no more stooping to see what's going on inside.

d *Flavour*
The food is cooked quickly, and ingredients such as fruit and vegetables are microwaved with the addition of very little liquid, leaving them bright in colour and full of flavour – the small loss of food value is an added bonus.

e *Re-heating*
This is quick, simple and excellent. Food, even cooked rice, really does re-heat perfectly. I would never advocate reheating cooked food by any other method, but with the microwave it really does taste as though it has just been cooked.

f *Drying herbs*
Simply spread the fresh herbs between sheets of absorbent kitchen paper and microwave on 100%/HIGH until dry. Make sure that you have a mug of water in the microwave when you dry herbs so that the water can take some of the microwave energy.

NOTES

The recipes given in this book were tested in a variable power model, the Philips M710, with an output of 700W. Please note that, should your oven be less powerful, you will have to increase the stated time according to the output of your oven. A rough guide would be to increase cooking times by 40 seconds per minute in a 500W oven and by 20 seconds per minute in a 600W oven. But remember that these times are intended as a guide only, and that it is better to undercook rather than overcook – you can always pop an undercooked meal back into the oven, but an overcooked one has already been spoiled. You will quickly get used to using the book in conjunction with your particular model.

Preparation time begins after the ingredients have been assembled.

Spoon measurements have been given as follows:

1 tbsp = 1 tablespoon = 15 ml
1 dstsp = 1 dessertspoon = 10 ml
1 tsp = 1 teaspoon = 5 ml

STARTERS

Tomato and Bramley soup
Smoked salmon dip
Carrot and lentil soup with dumplings
Cauliflower soup
Chick pea and walnut pâté
Carrot and parsnip soup
Scrambled eggs with tomatoes and prawns
Smoked haddock pâté
Beef and barley broth
Fennel and leeks with chestnuts
Chicken liver and almond pâté
Stilton dip
Curried rice and prawn starter
Cream of courgette soup
Artichokes with garlic mushroom sauce
Tomato and mushroom mousse
Macaroni in garlic cream sauce
Vegetable terrine
Mayonnaise and yoghurt sauce
Cheese and tuna flan
Potato and smoked mackerel bake
Curried plaice fillets

Many traditional starters include rather 'heavy' items, such as butter and double cream, in their lists of ingredients. These imaginative starters have been carefully compiled to produce eye-appealing results that are high on flavour but low on fat. Good use has been made of fresh vegetables and some of the recipes feature store-cupboard ingredients – ideal for the unexpected guest.

TOMATO AND BRAMLEY SOUP

A light, well-flavoured soup with vitamins A and C. The combined flavours of Bramley apple and ripe English tomatoes are unusual and delicious. Fresh basil adds a kick to this low-calorie, colourful soup. A summery British starter.

PREPARATION TIME: 30 minutes
MICROWAVE COOKING TIME: 20 minutes
SERVES: 4

675 g (1½ lb) ripe tomatoes, skinned and roughly chopped
1 small onion, chopped
1 medium-sized Bramley apple, peeled, cored and chopped
1 carrot, peeled and diced
juice and zest of ½ an orange
2 cloves garlic, peeled and chopped
30 g (1 oz) wholemeal flour
1 l (1¾ pt) well-flavoured chicken or vegetable stock, hot
salt and freshly ground black pepper
2 tsp finely chopped fresh basil or 1 tsp dried basil

TO SERVE
a few strips of orange peel, finely cut

1. Set the chopped tomatoes aside in a bowl.
2. Put the prepared onion, Bramley apple, carrot, orange juice and rind and the garlic into a large bowl or casserole. Cover and microwave on 100%/HIGH for 5 minutes, stirring and re-covering after 3 minutes.
3. Add the flour and stir well. Gradually add the hot stock,

stirring continuously. Season with a little salt and pepper. Add the basil and tomatoes and stir again.

4. Cover and microwave on 100%/HIGH for 15 minutes, stirring and re-covering after 6 minutes.
5. Allow to stand for 5 minutes, then pass through a sieve and serve garnished with some strips of orange peel.

SMOKED SALMON DIP

Smoked salmon is rich in calcium, protein and vitamins A and D and contains polyunsaturated fat. Here it is mixed with low-fat cottage cheese, yoghurt and oregano to produce a delicious dip. Serve with strips of carrot, celery and differently coloured peppers for a healthy starter. Scotch smoked salmon has the best flavour, but Irish is also good.

PREPARATION TIME: 5 minutes
MICROWAVE COOKING TIME: 3 minutes
SERVES: 6

1 small onion, chopped
1 small stick celery, finely chopped
85 g (3 oz) smoked salmon pieces
170 g (6 oz) cottage cheese
3 tbsp semi-skimmed milk
2 tbsp natural yoghurt
1 tsp dried oregano

1. Put the onion and celery into a soup or cereal bowl. Add 1 tbsp water. Cover and microwave on 100%/HIGH for 3 minutes. Stir and set aside.
2. Put the salmon pieces, cottage cheese, milk, yoghurt and oregano into a liquidizer or food processor. Process to blend. Add the onion and celery and process until smooth.
3. Turn into a serving dish. Cover and chill until ready to serve.

NOTE: A clove of garlic, peeled and chopped, may be added to the processor with the onion and celery if required.

CARROT AND LENTIL SOUP WITH DUMPLINGS

Carrots are an excellent source of vitamin A, the anti-infection vitamin, while lentils provide some protein. Both ingredients are high in fibre. A filling soup, which is low in fat. Almost a meal in itself!

PREPARATION TIME: 20 minutes
MICROWAVE COOKING TIME: 35 minutes
SERVES: 6

1 medium onion, chopped
2 cloves garlic, crushed
450 g (1 lb) carrots, peeled and diced
1 stick celery, chopped
85 g (3 oz) red split lentils, rinsed in cold water
397 g (14 oz) can chopped tomatoes
1 l (1¾ pt) vegetable stock, hot
salt and freshly ground black pepper

FOR THE DUMPLINGS
170 g (6 oz) wholemeal self-raising flour
55 g (2 oz) vegetable suet
1 tsp dried parsley
salt and freshly ground black pepper

TO SERVE
finely chopped parsley

1. Put the onion, garlic, carrots and celery into a large casserole. Cover and microwave for 5 minutes, stirring and re-covering after 3 minutes.
2. Stir in the lentils with the chopped tomatoes and the hot stock. Season. Cover and microwave on 70%/ROAST for 20 minutes, or until vegetables and lentils are cooked. Stir.
3. Set aside for 10 minutes.
4. Meanwhile prepare the dumplings. Put flour, suet and parsley into a bowl and add seasoning. Mix to a soft dough with 6–7 tbsp cold water. Form into 12 dumplings.
5. Arrange dumplings in a ring fashion on top of vegetables

and lentils. Cover and microwave on 100%/HIGH for 8–10 minutes. Serve immediately, sprinkled with a little extra finely chopped parsley.

An interesting traditional British recipe, which is naturally very healthy. The poor people looked to pulses to provide them with a cheap source of protein. They often used a small amount of smoked bacon with the lentils to add flavour.

CAULIFLOWER SOUP

A light but creamy soup, suitable for a dinner party. For trouble-free entertaining, this soup may be made earlier in the day and re-heated when your guests arrive.

PREPARATION TIME: 10 minutes
MICROWAVE COOKING TIME: 20 minutes
SERVES: 4

1 tbsp corn oil
1 small white cauliflower, florets only
1 small onion, chopped
570 ml (1 pt) light vegetable stock, warm
170 ml (6 fl oz) semi-skimmed milk
salt and freshly ground black pepper
1 level tbsp cornflour
115 ml (4 fl oz) Shape (reduced-fat) single cream
1 egg yolk

TO SERVE
finely chopped fresh parsley

1. Put oil into a large casserole and microwave, uncovered, for 30 seconds on 100%/HIGH.
2. Stir the cauliflower florets and the onion into the oil. Cover and microwave for 5 minutes on 100%/HIGH. Stir in 285 ml (½ pt) of the stock. Cover and microwave for 8 minutes, or until cauliflower is tender. Set aside for 5 minutes.

3. Carefully pour the contents of the casserole into a food processor or liquidizer and process until smooth. (Alternatively the ingredients may be sieved at this stage.)
4. Return processed ingredients to the large casserole. Add remaining stock and milk. Stir well and season. Cream cornflour to a smooth paste with a little milk and stir into casserole. Microwave, uncovered, stirring frequently, for 5–7 minutes on 100%/HIGH, or until soup boils and thickens. Set aside, covered, for 5 minutes.
5. Mix together the egg yolk and cream and stir into soup after its standing time.
6. Serve immediately, sprinkled with the finely chopped parsley.

Cauliflowers were introduced into this country in the seventeenth century and soon became one of the most popular of British vegetables. If cooking a whole cauliflower in the microwave, cook it upside-down in a covered casserole with 2 tbsp water.

CHICK PEA AND WALNUT PÂTÉ

This quick pâté with plenty of protein and flavour is made from canned chick peas. Serve on wholemeal toast with sticks of carrot, celery and cucumber.

PREPARATION TIME: 10 minutes
MICROWAVE COOKING TIME: 3 minutes
SERVES: 6–8

1 small onion, finely chopped
1 stick from celery heart, chopped
2 cloves garlic, chopped
432 g (15 oz) can chick peas, drained
5 g (2 oz) shelled walnuts, roughly chopped
3 tbsp olive oil
salt and freshly ground black pepper

TO GARNISH
fresh bayleaves

1. Put the onion, celery and garlic into a small casserole dish. Cover and microwave on 100%/HIGH for 3 minutes. Allow to stand for 2 minutes, then turn into liquidizer or food processor.
2. Add the drained chick peas and the walnuts. Process for about 3 seconds.
3. Add the oil and season with a little salt and some freshly ground black pepper. Process until blended.
4. Turn into an attractive pâté dish and level the surface.
5. Top with the bayleaves, then cover with clingfilm and refrigerate for at least an hour before serving.

Soaked split peas were often used to make pease pudding, another staple dish for the poor people in Victorian times.

CARROT AND PARSNIP SOUP

A healthy, low-fat soup. Carrots are a good source of vitamin A and they also contain some of the B group of vitamins, calcium and a little natural sugar. Parsnips contain carbohydrate and, therefore, provide energy. A well-flavoured soup to start any meal.

PREPARATION TIME: 15 minutes
MICROWAVE COOKING TIME: 25 minutes
SERVES: 4

1 medium onion, chopped
225 g (8 oz) carrots, peeled and diced
225 g (8 oz) parsnips, peeled and diced
1 clove garlic, crushed
570 ml (1 pt) well-flavoured chicken stock, cold
1 level tbsp finely chopped parsley
285 ml (½ pt) semi-skimmed milk
salt and freshly ground black pepper

TO SERVE
plenty of finely chopped parsley

1. Put the onions, carrots, parsnips and garlic into a large casserole. Add 2 tbsp stock.
2. Cover and microwave on 100%/HIGH for 6 minutes, stirring and re-covering after 3 minutes.
3. Carefully remove lid and add parsley, stock and milk. Season with a little salt and pepper. Stir well.
4. Cover and microwave on 100%/HIGH for 15 minutes, stirring and re-covering after 10 minutes.
5. Allow to stand for 10 minutes, then, using a draining spoon, lift vegetables into food processor or liquidizer. Add 285 ml (10 fl oz) of the liquid discarding the remainder. Liquidize or process until smooth.
6. Return puréed vegetables to casserole, stirring well. Cover and microwave for 3–4 minutes to re-heat.
7. Stir and serve, sprinkled with chopped parsley.

NOTE: If a liquidizer or food processor is not available, the vegetables may be sieved.

SCRAMBLED EGGS WITH TOMATOES AND PRAWNS

As eggs contain cholesterol in the yolk, they should be served no more than 3 times a week. However, they are high in protein, low in calories and a wonderful convenience food. Try this delicious recipe, served on wholemeal toast, as an unusual starter or light lunch when unexpected guests arrive.

PREPARATION TIME: 5 minutes
MICROWAVE COOKING TIME: 8–10 minutes
SERVES: 3

115 g (4 oz) fresh or frozen peeled prawns
4 eggs, size 2
3 tbsp semi-skimmed milk
3 tomatoes, skinned and chopped
salt and freshly ground black pepper
1 tsp dried parsley

TO SERVE
sprigs of fresh parsley

1. If prawns are frozen, lay them out in a single layer on a side plate. Microwave on 30%/DEFROST for 3–4 minutes. Rearrange prawns once during this time. Set aside to complete defrosting (about 10 minutes). Do not discard any liquid.
2. Beat together the eggs and milk and pour into a large bowl. Add the chopped tomatoes and season with a little salt and some pepper. Add the dried parsley with the prawns and their liquid.
3. Microwave, uncovered, on 100%/HIGH for 2 minutes. Stir well with a balloon whisk. Microwave on 100%/HIGH for 3–4 minutes, or until light and fluffy.
4. Stir again with the balloon whisk.
5. Serve immediately on warm wholemeal toast, garnished with the sprigs of parsley.

NOTE: If preferred, a 99 g (3½ oz) can of tuna, well drained and flaked, may be substituted for the prawns.

SMOKED HADDOCK PÂTÉ

Medium-fat soft cheese is similar in taste and texture to full-fat cream cheese, but contains only 50 calories per 28 g (1 oz) compared with 125 calories per 28 g (1 oz) for full-fat cream cheese. A starter with plenty of protein and calcium. Serve with warm wholemeal toast.

PREPARATION TIME: 10 minutes
MICROWAVE COOKING TIME: 5 minutes
SERVES: 4

225 g (8 oz) smoked haddock fillet
grated rind and juice of ½ lemon
1 clove garlic, crushed
1 tbsp horseradish sauce
1 tsp tomato purée
1 tbsp freshly chopped parsley
115 g (4 oz) medium-fat soft cheese

TO SERVE
side salad garnish
wedges of fresh lemon

1. Arrange the fish in a shallow dish in a single layer. Add the grated lemon rind and juice. Cover and microwave on 100%/HIGH for 4 minutes. Set aside until cool.
2. Put the crushed garlic and the horseradish into a liquidizer or food processor. Add the tomato purée and the chopped parsley. Flake in the cooled haddock with the soft cheese and any fish juices, but discard the skin.
3. Liquidize or process until smooth.
4. Turn into a pâté dish and level the surface. Chill until ready to serve.
5. Serve garnished with a side salad and wedges of lemon. Hand warm toast round separately.

Smoked haddock originated in Scotland, where crofters smoked the fish over smouldering fires in their cottages. It should always be cooked before eating. Look out for browny gold fillets of fish, which represent haddock at its best.

Beef and Barley Broth

This warming winter soup makes a little beef go a long way. Filling and nutritious with plenty of fibre. Serve with home-made wholemeal bread and a vegetable pâté to make the soup into a main meal. Remember to soak the dried peas in water overnight.

PREPARATION TIME: 25 minutes
MICROWAVE COOKING TIME: 1 hour 50 minutes
SERVES: 8

340 g (12 oz) stewing steak, diced, all visible fat removed
3 beef stock cubes
115 g (4 oz) pearl barley
115 g (4 oz) dried peas, soaked in water overnight
1 tbsp dried mixed herbs
salt and freshly ground black pepper
1 medium onion, finely chopped
2 large courgettes, diced
1 small turnip, peeled and diced
2 large carrots, peeled and diced
2 medium potatoes, peeled and diced
115 g (4 oz) red cabbage, shredded
397 g (14 oz) can chopped tomatoes
1.7 l (3 pt) boiling water

1. Put the beef into a very large casserole.
2. Add the pearl barley, dried peas (which have been soaked overnight, then drained), the mixed herbs and seasoning, the onion, courgettes, turnip, carrots, potatoes and the red cabbage. Stir.
3. Add the tomatoes with the crumbled stock cubes and carefully pour over the boiling water. Stir well until stock cubes have dissolved. Cover and microwave on 100%/HIGH for 20 minutes or until boiling.
4. Carefully stir and re-cover.
5. Microwave on 40%/SIMMER for 1½ hours, stirring and re-covering 3 times.
6. Stir and allow to stand for 10 minutes before serving.

Pearl barley is the polished, steamed grain of a cereal grass. It has been used for centuries to thicken soups and stews and is also used in barley water.

FENNEL AND LEEKS WITH CHESTNUTS

A highly nutritious starter, which is full of fibre and also provides protein and a little fat. Serve with wholemeal toast or scones for an inexpensive and different start to a special meal.

PREPARATION TIME: 7 minutes
MICROWAVE COOKING TIME: 16 minutes
SERVES: 4

2 large leeks, cleaned and sliced
2 medium heads fennel, trimmed and sliced
150 ml (¼ pt) vegetable stock
227 g (8 oz) can whole chestnuts, drained
85 g (3 oz) button mushrooms, sliced
3 tbsp grated Parmesan

1. Put the prepared leeks and fennel into a large shallow dish. Pour over the stock.
2. Cover and microwave on 100%/HIGH for 12 minutes, stirring and re-covering after 5 minutes. Remove cover. Baste with stock. Return to microwave on 100%/HIGH for 2 minutes, uncovered, to reduce stock. Add the chestnuts and mushrooms. Stir. Cover and microwave on 100%/HIGH for 2 minutes.
3. Remove cover. Top evenly with grated Parmesan and brown under a grill before serving.

Chestnuts were gathered wild and were frequently boiled or roasted and often served with game or poultry.

CHICKEN LIVER AND ALMOND PÂTÉ

Protein is provided in both the chicken livers and the ground almonds. A delicious combination of flavours. The low-fat spread contains about half the calories of butter or margarine. Serve with freshly made toast.

PREPARATION TIME: 15 minutes
MICROWAVE COOKING TIME: 7 minutes
SERVES: 4

225 g (8 oz) chicken livers
1 rasher streaky bacon, de-rinded and chopped
1 clove garlic, crushed
salt and freshly ground black pepper
55 g (2 oz) ground almonds
85 g (3 oz) low-fat spread
1 tbsp chopped parsley
2 tbsp milk

TO SERVE
parsley sprigs
crudités

1. Pick over the chicken livers and discard any membranes.
2. Put the chicken livers, chopped bacon and garlic into a medium-sized bowl or casserole. Season lightly with salt and pepper. Cover and microwave on 70%/ROAST for 5 minutes, stirring and re-covering after 2 minutes. Stir and set aside to cool, then stir in the ground almonds. Transfer to a liquidizer or food processor.
3. Put the low-fat spread into a bowl and microwave on 70%/ROAST for 1½–2 minutes, or until melted.
4. Pour into the liquidizer or food processor and add the parsley and milk. Liquidize or process until smooth.
5. Turn into pâté dish and refrigerate until set.
6. Serve garnished with parsley sprigs, with freshly made toast and crudités.

In Georgian England, pâtés became particularly popular and many contrasting ingredients were used. When formulating this recipe I liked the texture, and the flavour of the ground almonds combined with the chicken livers.

STILTON DIP

A little Stilton cheese goes a long way, as it has a wonderfully rich taste. In this recipe it is combined with natural yoghurt and reduced-calorie mayonnaise to make a delicious starter.

PREPARATION TIME: 10 minutes
MICROWAVE COOKING TIME: nil
SERVES: 4

85 g (3oz) Stilton cheese, crumbled
150 ml (1/4 pt) reduced-calorie mayonnaise
salt and freshly ground black pepper
3 tbsp natural set yoghurt
1 clove garlic, crushed
2 tbsp soured cream
1 tsp horseradish sauce
1 stick celery, finely chopped

TO SERVE
vegetable sticks
crisps

1. Put the Stilton into a food processor or liquidizer.
2. Add the mayonnaise, seasoning, natural yoghurt, garlic, soured cream and horseradish. Process to combine.
3. Stir in chopped celery and turn into serving dish.
4. Serve surrounded by freshly made vegetable sticks and crisps.

CURRIED RICE AND PRAWN STARTER

Prawns add protein and a touch of delicious luxury to this unusual starter.

PREPARATION TIME: 15 minutes
MICROWAVE COOKING TIME: 9–10 minutes
SERVES: 4

115 g (4 oz) fresh or frozen peeled prawns
115 g (4 oz) long-grain rice
1 tsp curry powder
340 ml (12 fl oz) boiling water
55 g (2 oz) frozen peas
99 g (3½ oz) can tuna fish, drained and flaked
1 tsp lemon juice
3 tbsp reduced-calorie mayonnaise
salt and freshly ground black pepper

TO SERVE
salad garnish
twist of lemon

1. If the prawns are frozen, defrost in the microwave (see p.27).
2. Put rice into a 1.7 l (3 pt) bowl. Add curry powder and season.
3. Carefully pour on boiling water, cover and microwave on 100%/HIGH for 9–10 minutes. Stand, covered, for 5 minutes. Fork up, adding peas. Set aside until cold.
4. In a large mixing bowl combine the prawns and tuna fish, the lemon juice, the cooled curried rice and the reduced-calorie mayonnaise. Adjust seasoning, then mix well to combine.
5. Arrange a salad garnish on each of 4 side plates, then spoon on rice mixture attractively. Garnish with a twist of lemon and serve immediately.

CREAM OF COURGETTE SOUP

This is an easy soup which is low in calories as no fat is used in the recipe. A high-fibre starter with plenty of creamy flavour.

PREPARATION TIME: 5 minutes
MICROWAVE COOKING TIME: 20 minutes
SERVES: 4

1 small onion, chopped
450 g (1 lb) fresh courgettes, topped, tailed and sliced
150 ml (¼ pt) light chicken stock
570 ml (1 pt) semi-skimmed milk
2 tsp freshly chopped thyme
salt and freshly ground black pepper

1. Put the onion into a large mixing bowl or casserole. Add the courgettes with the stock. Cover and microwave on 100%/HIGH for 10–12 minutes. Stand for 5 minutes.

2. Turn contents of bowl into food processor or liquidizer and process until smooth. Return to bowl. Stir in milk and thyme. Season and cover.
3. Microwave on 100%/HIGH for about 7 minutes, or until boiling. Stir twice during this time.
4. Serve immediately.

Courgettes (or baby marrows) are also known as zucchini. As this name suggests, they originated in Italy, but the British marrow has been with us for centuries. Mrs Beeton in her book *All About Cookery* gives many recipes for marrow, among them marrow jam, pickled marrow and marrow preserve.

ARTICHOKES WITH GARLIC MUSHROOM SAUCE

Globe artichokes are in season from June to September. They supply fibre and a little vitamin C. Choose young, fresh heads, allowing one per person. They are cooked when the leaves detach easily when gently pulled.

PREPARATION TIME: 7 minutes
MICROWAVE COOKING TIME: 17–20 minutes
SERVES: 3

3 globe artichokes, stalks cut off level with leaves
1 tsp lemon juice

FOR THE SAUCE
30 g (1 oz) low-fat spread
30 g (1 oz) flour
285 ml (½ pt) semi-skimmed milk
2 cloves garlic, crushed
225 g (8 oz) button mushrooms, chopped

1. Remove the stalk and hard base leaves from each artichoke and cut ¼″ off the top leaves with scissors. Wash well and soak for 1 hour in cold water. Drain.

2. Put the prepared artichokes, points downwards, into a large dish. Add 4 tbsp water and the lemon juice and cover. Microwave on 100%/HIGH for 10–12 minutes.
3. Set aside, covered, while preparing the sauce.
4. Put the low-fat spread, flour, milk and garlic into a large jug or medium-sized mixing bowl.
5. Microwave, uncovered, on 100%/HIGH for 3–4 minutes, stirring with a wire balloon whisk every minute. The sauce must boil rapidly and thicken.
6. Stir in the mushrooms and return to the microwave, covered. Microwave on 40%/SIMMER for 4 minutes.
7. Drain the artichokes and place in serving-dish. Offer the sauce separately.

The correct way to eat artichoke is to pull out the leaves, one at a time, and dip the soft end in the sauce before eating it. In the centre of each artichoke is the soft flowery part or choke. Eat the bottom of this, which is delicious, with a knife and fork.

Tomato and Mushroom Mousse

A light starter, providing vitamins B and C. Low in calories and high on flavour, this mousse should be served with wholemeal toast.

PREPARATION TIME: 10 minutes
MICROWAVE COOKING TIME: 5 minutes
SERVES: 4

30 g (1 oz) low-fat spread
170 g (6 oz) button mushrooms, finely chopped
3 tomatoes, skinned and chopped
1 tbsp finely chopped parsley
1 clove garlic, crushed
salt and freshly ground black pepper
1 11 g (0.4 oz) sachet gelatine
85 ml (3 fl oz) low-calorie salad dressing (oil-free)
2 eggs, size 3, separated

TO GARNISH
cherry tomato
sprigs of parsley

1. Put the low-fat spread and the mushrooms into a small casserole dish. Cover and microwave on 100%/HIGH for 3 minutes, stirring and re-covering after 1½ minutes. Set aside.
2. Stir in the tomatoes, parsley and garlic. Season lightly.
3. Sprinkle the gelatine over 2 tbsp water in a soup or cereal bowl. Set aside for 5 minutes, then microwave on 40%/SIMMER for 2 minutes. Stir to ensure gelatine has dissolved.
4. Beat the egg yolks into the salad dressing in a fairly large mixing bowl. Fold in the tomato/mushroom mixture.
5. Stir in the dissolved gelatine. Refrigerate until just starting to set (5–10 minutes).
6. Whisk the egg whites until stiff and fold into tomato/mushroom mixture.
7. Spoon into individual dishes and refrigerate until set.
8. Decorate with a ring cut from a cherry tomato and a sprig of parsley. Serve with wholemeal toast.

MACARONI IN GARLIC CREAM SAUCE

Macaroni cheese is a basic traditional 'standby' which can be rather boring. Try this delicious pasta recipe, which uses light *fromage frais* in the sauce instead of the usual hard cheese. Carbohydrate, protein and fat are supplied in this recipe, which may be served as a starter or for a light lunch.

PREPARATION TIME: 10 minutes
MICROWAVE COOKING TIME: 14–17 minutes
SERVES: 4

225 g (8 oz) short-cut macaroni
1 tsp olive oil

FOR THE SAUCE
1 onion, finely chopped
1 clove garlic, chopped
170 g (6 oz) *fromage frais*
115 g (4 oz) lean ham, diced
30 ml (1 fl oz) milk
55 g (2 oz) grated Parmesan cheese

TO GARNISH
a few sprigs of parsley

1. Put the macaroni into a 2.8 l (5 pt) casserole. Pour over a kettle of boiling water. Add the oil.
2. Cover and microwave on 100%/HIGH for 10–12 minutes, stirring and re-covering once, halfway through cooking, using the handle of a wooden spoon.
3. Set aside, covered, for 5 minutes while preparing the sauce, then drain and rinse with plenty of boiling water.
4. Prepare the sauce. Put the onion into a medium-sized casserole. Cover and microwave on 100%/HIGH for 2 minutes. Stir in the garlic. Add the *fromage frais* with the ham. Gradually blend in the milk.
5. Cover and microwave on 40%/SIMMER for 2–3 minutes, stirring and re-covering after 2 minutes. Stir again when cooked.
6. Turn the macaroni on to a warmed serving dish. Top with the prepared sauce and serve immediately, sprinkled with plenty of Parmesan cheese, and garnished with sprigs of fresh parsley.

Macaroni has always been a good store-cupboard ingredient. Between the two world wars it was widely used for sweet and savoury dishes and then, probably due to its over-use, went out of fashion. Today there is such a wide variety of pasta shapes available that good old dependable macaroni is often overlooked.

VEGETABLE TERRINE

This well-flavoured, attractive layered dish is served cut into slices and accompanied by wholemeal toast and a salad garnish. A delicious combination of puréed English vegetables, garlic and cottage cheese provides a meal that is full of fibre, protein and a little fat. Ideal on a buffet table. Serve with mayonnaise and yoghurt sauce (see p. 39).

PREPARATION TIME: 30 minutes
MICROWAVE COOKING TIME: 48 minutes
SERVES: 8

1 medium onion, chopped
450 g (1 lb) carrots, peeled and sliced
3 cloves garlic, chopped individually
½ tsp celery seasoning
450 g (1 lb) parsnips, peeled and diced
450 g (1 lb) frozen sliced courgettes
3 eggs, size 3
salt and freshly ground black pepper
115 g (4 oz) fresh brown breadcrumbs
170 g (6 oz) cottage cheese
3 tbsp milk

1. Put the prepared onion and carrots into a round casserole with 2 tbsp water. Add 1 clove chopped garlic and the celery seasoning. Cover and microwave on 100%/HIGH for 9 minutes. Stir, re-cover and set aside.
2. Put the parsnips into another round casserole with 2 tbsp water. Add 1 clove chopped garlic.
3. Cover and microwave on 100%/HIGH for 9 minutes. Stir, re-cover and set aside.
4. Put the frozen courgettes into a third round casserole. Add garlic but do not add water. Cover and microwave on 100%/HIGH for 10 minutes, stirring and re-covering after 4 minutes. Set aside, covered.
5. Using the metal blade, turn the carrots into a food processor or liquidizer with any cooking liquid. Process until very

finely chopped. Add 1 egg and a little black pepper, with 55 g (2 oz) breadcrumbs and 55 g (2 oz) cottage cheese. Process until smooth. Turn this mixture into a very lightly oiled 1.7 l (3 pt) oblong microwave bread baker. Spread out evenly.

6. Wash up food processor, then place in it the parsnips and any liquid. Process until smooth. Add milk, 1 egg and seasoning and process again. Add 55 g (2 oz) cottage cheese and 55 g (2 oz) breadcrumbs. Process again until smooth.
7. Turn parsnip mixture on to carrot mixture. Spread out evenly to form a second layer.
8. Wash up food processor. Put courgettes and any liquid into the processor and process until smooth. Add 1 egg and seasoning and process again. Add remaining cottage cheese. Process again until smooth.
9. Turn courgette mixture on to parsnip layer. Spread out evenly.
10. Cover with polyethylene clingfilm, pierce the cling film once and microwave on 40%/SIMMER for 20 minutes, or until set. Allow to stand until cool. Chill until ready to serve.
11. Turn out and serve cut into slices, accompanied by the mayonnaise and yoghurt sauce.

NOTE: It may be necessary to stop the food processor or liquidizer during processing, remove food from sides with a spatula and then continue to process.

Take care when microwaving the terrine on 40%/SIMMER, as different microwaves may differ in time taken to set the dish.

MAYONNAISE AND YOGHURT SAUCE

Mayonnaise made from olive oil and eggs is delicious but can be rather rich. The addition of freshly chopped parsley and yoghurt lightens the mayonnaise and turns it into a delicious sauce, which complements the terrine.

PREPARATION TIME: 10 minutes
MICROWAVE COOKING TIME: Nil
SERVES: 6–8

1 egg, size 3
1 egg yolk
285 ml (½ pt) olive oil
salt and freshly ground black pepper
1 tbsp freshly chopped parsley
grated rind of ½ lemon
140 ml (5 fl oz) carton natural yoghurt

1. Put the egg and the egg yolk into a food processor or liquidizer. Process for a few seconds. (Use the metal blade on a food processor.)
2. With the machine running, add the oil, a drop at a time to start with, then more quickly, until a thick mayonnaise results. Add the seasoning and the chopped parsley. Process again for a few seconds.
3. Add the lemon rind and natural yoghurt and process to combine.
4. Pour into serving dish and chill until ready to serve.

Mayonnaise has been popular in this country since the middle of the nineteenth century. Mrs Beeton suggests adding a teaspoon of French mustard with the eggs, and this does seem to help to ensure that the resulting mayonnaise is really thick. Try it, it will complement the Vegetable Terrine well.

CHEESE AND TUNA FLAN

Although the cheese and egg flan as we know it originated in France, it has become very popular in this country, where it is served as a starter or light supper dish. Try this fish version, and note how well the pastry works in the microwave.

PREPARATION TIME: 30 minutes
MICROWAVE COOKING TIME: 20 minutes
SERVES: 4–6

FOR THE PASTRY
85 g (3 oz) polyunsaturated margarine at room temperature
115 g (4 oz) plain flour
55 g (2 oz) wholemeal flour } **sieved together**

FOR THE FILLING
1 small onion, chopped
2 eggs, size 2
140 ml (¼ pt) semi-skimmed milk
1 tsp dried parsley
seasoning
99 g (3½ oz) can tuna fish drained
55 g (2 oz) low-fat Cheddar-type cheese

TO SERVE
a little paprika pepper

1. Put the margarine with 2 tbsp water into a medium-sized mixing bowl.
2. Whip up with a fork. Add one-third of the flour and mix with a fork to combine. Add remaining flour and mix again to form a dough. Knead lightly.
3. Refrigerate for 20 minutes.
4. Roll dough out and use to line an 18 cm (7″) microwave flan dish.
5. Using a fork, prick over sides and base of flan dish.
6. Lay one sheet or absorbent kitchen paper in base of flan and microwave on 100%/HIGH for 3 minutes.
7. Remove paper and continue to microwave on 100%/HIGH for 2 minutes. Allow to stand for 5 minutes.
8. Prepare the filling. Put the chopped onion into a medium-sized mixing bowl. Cover and microwave on 100%/HIGH for 1½ minutes.
9. Whisk together the eggs, milk, parsley and seasoning and pour over the onion. Stir. Microwave on 70%/ROAST for 3 minutes, stirring every minute.
10. Drain the tuna fish and flake it evenly over the cooked flan base. Top with the grated cheese.

11. Pour the warmed egg mixture into the flan.
12. Microwave on 70%/ROAST for 8–10 minutes, or until filling is set. Sprinkle with paprika pepper. Serve warm or cold.

NOTE: It is important that the margarine is at room temperature for this recipe.

POTATO AND SMOKED MACKEREL BAKE

A nutritious and filling starter. Vitamin C is provided in the potatoes. The fish contains polyunsaturated fat and plenty of protein. A delicious combination of flavours.

PREPARATION TIME: 40 minutes
MICROWAVE COOKING TIME: 34 minutes
SERVES: 4

1 small onion, chopped
565 g (1 lb 4oz) potatoes, scrubbed clean and sliced thinly
175 g (6 oz) smoked mackerel fillet, flaked

FOR THE SAUCE
30 g (1 oz) vegetable margarine
30 g (1 oz) flour
1 l (1¾ pt) semi-skimmed milk
85 g (3 oz) cottage cheese
seasoning
½ tsp made mustard
55 g (2 oz) grated low-fat Cheddar-type cheese
55 g (2 oz) fresh brown breadcrumbs

TO GARNISH
a few mixed salad ingredients

1. Put the onion into a soup or cereal bowl. Cover and microwave on 100%/HIGH for 1 minute.
2. In 4 cereal bowls layer the potatoes, onion and flaked mackerel evenly, starting and finishing with a layer of potato.

3. Make the sauce. Put the margarine in a litre (2 pt) jug and microwave on 100%/HIGH for 30 seconds–1 minute, or until melted and hot. Stir in the flour, then gradually add the milk, stirring.
4. Microwave, uncovered, on 100%/HIGH for about 4 minutes, beating with a balloon whisk every minute. The sauce must rise right up in the jug and thicken.
5. Stir in the seasoning, mustard and cottage cheese.
6. Divide the sauce between the 4 cereal bowls, pouring it over the potatoes evenly.
7. Cover each bowl with polyethylene clingfilm and pierce it once or twice.
8. Microwave all the bowls together on 70%/ROAST for 23 minutes. Turn bowls after 12 minutes. Allow to stand for 5 minutes.
9. Remove clingfilm. Combine breadcrumbs and cheese and divide evenly between bowls, sprinkling it over.
10. Microwave all bowls together on 100%/HIGH, uncovered, for 5 minutes.
11. Serve immediately with a salad garnish.

This is a lighter version of a delicious Irish starter served to my niece in a restaurant in Winchester, which prides itself on its traditional British fare.

CURRIED PLAICE FILLETS

Serve one fish fillet per person for an unusual healthy starter. The vegetable curry filling is delicious. Hand the bowl of sauce round separately. Warm granary rolls are a good accompaniment to this starter.

PREPARATION TIME: 15 minutes
MICROWAVE COOKING TIME: 6 minutes
SERVES: 4

4 plaice fillets
1 courgette, grated
1 onion, chopped
1 medium tomato, skinned and chopped
1 tsp curry powder
30 g (1 oz) mushrooms, chopped
30 g (1 oz) raisins
30 g (1 oz) fresh brown breadcrumbs
30 g (1 oz) vegetable margarine

FOR THE CURRY SAUCE
140 ml (5 fl oz) soured cream
2 tbsp semi-skimmed milk
1 tsp tomato purée
1 tsp curry powder
1 tbsp low-calorie salad cream
freshly ground black pepper

TO SERVE
very lightly cooked sticks of courgette and carrot

1. Prepare the filling for the plaice. Put the grated courgette and the chopped onion into a medium-sized bowl.
2. Cover and microwave on 100%/HIGH for 2½ minutes.
3. Add the chopped tomato, the curry powder, the mushrooms, raisins and fresh breadcrumbs. Stir to combine.
4. Divide filling evenly between plaice fillets and spread over evenly. Roll fish up, head to tail, and arrange all 4 fillets in a circle in a shallow dish.
5. Divide the margarine into 4 pieces and put one on each fillet.
6. Cover with polyethylene clingfilm, pierce it once or twice and microwave on 100%/HIGH for about 3½ minutes. Allow to stand for 2 minutes.
7. Serve 1 fillet per person with a few crudités and hand the curry sauce around separately.

TO PREPARE THE CURRY SAUCE
Simply combine all ingredients and refrigerate until ready to serve.

The traditional English fashion of serving fresh fish was to serve it plain, that is, without rich and exotic sauces. This sauce, made with soured cream and served with the poached fish and vegetable crudités, adds interest to the meal.

MAIN MEALS

Chicken cutlets
Chilli prawns
Apricot chicken
Macaroni cheese
Garden casserole
Lambs' liver layer
Beef in beer
Pork with ginger and cabbage
Cheese, onion and parsley pudding
Chicken livers with new potatoes
Shepherd's pie
Braised pork
Bacon-and-walnut-stuffed chicken
Turkey breasts in tomato sauce
Chicken breasts in cheese sauce
Lamb curry
Lamb's liver with vegetables
Meat loaf ring
Kedgeree
Vegetarian rice
Tomatoes with monkfish

CHICKEN CUTLETS

A healthy version of traditional chicken cutlets. These are fried in a little oil in a microwave browning dish. A good way to use up any left-over chicken. These crisp cutlets are very popular with children. Serve with a mixed salad.

PREPARATION TIME: 20 minutes
MICROWAVE COOKING TIME: 19 minutes
SERVES: Makes 6 cutlets

340 g (12 oz) potatoes, peeled and diced
4 tbsp milk
225 g (8 oz) cold chicken meat, minced or chopped
1 tbsp frozen sweetcorn
1 tbsp frozen peas
1 tbsp quick-cooking oats
salt and freshly ground black pepper
1 egg, beaten
85 g (3 oz) fresh brown breadcrumbs
2 tbsp corn oil

TO SERVE
mixed salad

1. Put the diced potato into a medium-sized casserole or mixing bowl. Add 2 tbsp milk. Cover and microwave on 100%/HIGH for 7 minutes. Stir and set aside for 5 minutes.
2. Mash down the potatoes, adding remaining milk. Whip with a fork. Add the chicken, sweetcorn, peas and oats. Mix well and season.
3. Form into 6 cutlets when cool and coat carefully with egg and then breadcrumbs. Refrigerate for 20 minutes, if at all possible.
4. Pre-heat a large browning dish without its lid on 100%/HIGH for 7 minutes.
5. Put the oil into the hot dish, tipping the dish so that it coats the base. Microwave for 1 minute on 100%/HIGH. Put the cutlets into the dish.
6. Microwave, uncovered, on 100%/HIGH for 2 minutes.

7. Turn each cutlet over and continue to microwave on 100%/HIGH for 2 minutes. Serve immediately with a mixed salad.

CHILLI PRAWNS

Green chillis are used in this main-meal recipe, which is definitely not for the faint-hearted! A delightful dinner-party recipe, which is quick and easy to prepare. Cook some Basmati rice in the microwave a little earlier, and re-heat it when your guests are ready to eat.

PREPARATION TIME: 10 minutes
MICROWAVE COOKING TIME: 21 minutes
SERVES: 4

450 g (1 lb) fresh or frozen peeled prawns
2 tbsp sunflower oil
1 medium onion, finely chopped
2 green chillis, deseeded and chopped
2 cloves garlic, crushed
170 g (6 oz) button mushrooms, sliced
400 g (14 oz) can chopped tomatoes
1 tbsp freshly chopped parsley
salt and freshly ground black pepper

TO SERVE
plenty of freshly chopped parsley
cooked Basmati rice
green salad

1. If the prawns are frozen, defrost in the microwave for 7–8 minutes (see p. 27).
2. Pre-heat a large, deep, microwave browning dish without its lid for 7 minutes on 100%/HIGH.
3. Pour in the oil and microwave, uncovered, on 100%/HIGH for 1 minute. Stir in the onion, chillis and garlic. Cover and microwave on 100%/HIGH for 2 minutes. Stir in the mushrooms. Cover and microwave on 100%/HIGH for 2 minutes.
4. Stir in the tomatoes and the parsley. Season. Cover and

microwave on 100%/HIGH for 5 minutes, stirring and re-covering after 3 minutes. Stir in the prawns, season, cover and microwave on 100%/HIGH for 3–4 minutes, stirring after 2 minutes.

5. Serve immediately on a bed of steaming Basmati rice, sprinkled with the chopped parsley and accompanied by a green salad. Also delicious served cold.

Looking through old cookery books I found several recipes for curried prawns. For a change I decided to include my recipe for chilli prawns, which, in fact, I first tasted in Thailand, where they eat very spicy food. It was cooked for me with far more chillis and garlic than suggested here. I adapted it to suit my palate and I hope that it suits yours, too. I often cook it for unexpected guests. Serve a dry white wine or lager with the meal.

APRICOT CHICKEN

Devilled chicken with fruit is a spicy, low-fat, high-protein dish, which is ideal served as a treat for the family but is also suitable for entertaining. Serve with scalloped potatoes and a green vegetable such as courgettes.

PREPARATION TIME: 20 minutes plus soaking and marinading time
MICROWAVE COOKING TIME: 19 minutes
SERVES: 4

8 dried apricots, soaked (see step 1)
4 skinned and boned chicken breasts, total weight 450 g (1 lb)

FOR THE MARINADE
1 tbsp Worcestershire sauce
2 tsp anchovy sauce
1 clove garlic, crushed
½ tsp dried oregano
2 tbsp soya sauce
1 tbsp olive oil

TO COMPLETE THE DISH
1 tbsp olive oil
1 medium onion, chopped
3 tsp cornflour
115 g (4 oz) frozen peas, defrosted

TO SERVE
55 g (2 oz) toasted flaked almonds (see note)

1. Put the dried apricots into a large bowl. Cover with 285 ml (½ pt) boiling water. Cover and leave on one side for 1½ hours.
2. After soaking, drain apricots. Re-cover with 285 ml (½ pt) boiling water. Cover with polyethylene clingfilm, pierce it once or twice and microwave on 100%/HIGH for 7 minutes. Set aside.
3. Meanwhile prepare the chicken. Cut the breasts into thin strips and lay them in a single layer in a suitable dish.
4. Combine all ingredients for the marinade and pour over the chicken. Cover with a lid and refrigerate for at least 2 hours, turning the chicken in the marinade at least twice during this time.
5. To complete the dish, put the oil and onion into a large casserole and microwave on 100%/HIGH for 2 minutes. Stir in the chicken with its marinade. Cover and microwave on 100%/HIGH for 5 minutes, stirring and re-covering after 3 minutes.
6. Stir in the cooked chopped apricots with their juice.
7. Cream the cornflour to a smooth paste with a little water and stir into the casserole. Microwave, uncovered, stirring frequently, on 100%/HIGH for 5 minutes, or until sauce boils and thickens. Stir in peas.
8. Serve immediately, garnished with the toasted flaked almonds.

NOTE: The flaked almonds may be toasted in the microwave. Simply spread them out on a dinner plate and microwave, uncovered, stirring frequently until lightly browned. 55 g (2 oz) will take about 4 minutes in a 700 W microwave.

'Devilling' means, simply, treating pieces of meat or poultry with hot spicy ingredients so that they penetrate into the foods, which are then cooked and eaten hot or cold.

MACARONI CHEESE

Macaroni cheese has always been a store-cupboard 'standby'. This recipe uses crisp brown breadcrumbs to line the base of the dish, and the sauce is flavoured with onion, cheese and mustard. Use semi-skimmed milk to keep the fat content of the recipe down and serve with a fresh green salad.

PREPARATION TIME: 20 minutes
MICROWAVE COOKING TIME: 15 minutes
SERVES: 4

170 g (6 oz) short-cut macaroni, quick-cooking variety
45 g (1½ oz) vegetable margarine
1 small onion, chopped
30 g (1 oz) plain flour
salt and freshly ground black pepper
½ tsp mustard powder
570 ml (1 pt) semi-skimmed milk
170 g (6 oz) grated Cheddar cheese
115 g (4 oz) toasted brown breadcrumbs (see note)

TO SERVE
1 sliced tomato
sprigs of parsley

1. Put the macaroni into a really large casserole, about 3.4 l (6 pt) capacity.
2. Pour over a kettle full of boiling water. Cover and microwave on 100%/HIGH for 4 minutes. Set aside, covered, for 5 minutes.
3. Put the margarine and onion into a large mixing bowl, about 2.3 l (4 pt) capacity.
4. Cover and microwave on 100%/HIGH for 2 minutes.

5. Stir in the flour, blending well. Season and add the mustard powder. Stir in the milk.
6. Microwave, uncovered, stirring frequently on 100%/HIGH for 4–6 minutes, or until sauce boils and thickens.
7. Stir in 85 g (3 oz) of the cheese.
8. Drain the macaroni after its standing time and rinse with plenty of boiling water.
9. Put 55 g (2 oz) of the crisp brown breadcrumbs into a suitable serving dish. Top with the macaroni. Pour the cheese sauce over to coat.
10. Sprinkle remaining toasted breadcrumbs evenly over the cheese sauce. Top with the rest of the cheese.
11. Return to the microwave, uncovered, for about 3 minutes on 100%/HIGH to heat through, then serve immediately, garnished with slices of tomato and sprigs of parsley.

NOTE: The breadcrumbs are quick and easy to prepare – simply crumb the bread either by machine or hand, then line the tray of the grill pan, turned upside-down, with foil. Sprinkle the breadcrumbs evenly on to the foil and brown under the grill, turning frequently until golden.

GARDEN CASSEROLE

Lambs' kidneys are marinaded in oil, fruit juice and garlic and then cooked with traditional vegetables and beef stock to produce a delicious stew. Just before serving, red kidney beans are added and the cooked casserole is sprinkled with cubes of wholemeal bread and browned under the grill. A warming, traditional beef casserole.

PREPARATION TIME: 20 minutes plus marinading time
MICROWAVE COOKING TIME: 1 hour 34 minutes
SERVES: 4

225 g (8 oz) lambs' kidneys, cored and chopped
450 g (1 lb) lean chuck steak, cubed
2 rashers back bacon, de-rinded and chopped

FOR THE MARINADE
1 small onion, chopped
1 clove garlic, crushed
2 tbsp corn oil
285 ml (½ pt) pure apple juice
1 bayleaf or sprig of mint, 1 piece of rosemary
salt and freshly ground black pepper

FOR THE CASSEROLE
1 large onion, sliced
1 stick celery, chopped
2 carrots, peeled and sliced
1 courgette, sliced
1 rounded tbsp wholemeal flour
140 ml (¼ pt) well-flavoured beef stock, hot
2 tbsp tomato purée
432 g (15 oz) can red kidney beans, drained
2 large slices wholemeal bread, cubed

TO SERVE
plenty of freshly chopped parsley

1. Put the cubed steak and prepared kidney with the bacon into a suitable dish.
2. Mix together all the ingredients for the marinade and whisk with a fork to combine. Pour over the meat. Cover and set aside for 1–2 hours, turning the meat in the marinade every hour. (Leave overnight in the fridge if preferred.)
3. Put the onion, celery, carrots and courgette into a fairly large casserole. Cover and microwave on 100%/HIGH for 5 minutes. Stir.
4. Using a draining spoon, lift meat from marinade and, retaining marinade, add meat to vegetables. Cover and microwave on 100%/HIGH for 7 minutes. Stir. Stir in flour, then add reserved marinade, tomato purée and the hot beef stock. Stir well.
5. Cover and microwave on 100%/HIGH for 8–10 minutes, or until boiling. Stir. Re-cover and microwave on 40%/SIMMER for 1 hour 10 minutes, stirring and re-covering twice during this time. Allow to stand, covered, for 10 minutes.
6. Add the drained kidney beans. Cover and microwave on 100%/HIGH for 1–2 minutes to heat beans through.

7. Sprinkle cubed bread over the cooked stew, then brown under the grill before serving sprinkled with plenty of freshly chopped parsley.

We are very fortunate that many pulses such as red kidney beans, chick peas and butter beans are now available in cans. Although they are far more expensive in this form, it does cut out cooking them, which, even in the microwave, is rather time-consuming!

LAMBS' LIVER LAYER

An ideal way of cooking the complete meal in one dish. Little washing-up afterwards and plenty of flavour in this nutritious main meal. Liver provides protein, iron, vitamin A, vitamin B complex and iron. Potatoes provide carbohydrate and vitamin C. As liver, unfortunately, also contains cholesterol, it should be served only once a week.

PREPARATION TIME: 20 minutes
MICROWAVE COOKING TIME: 32 minutes
SERVES: 3

1 rasher back bacon, de-rinded and chopped
1 large onion, chopped
340 g (12 oz) lambs' liver slices
675 g (1½ lb) potatoes, peeled and thinly sliced
½ 397 g (14 oz) can chopped tomatoes
½ tsp dried oregano
salt and freshly ground black pepper
85 ml (3 fl oz) light beef stock

TO SERVE
a little paprika pepper

1. Put the chopped bacon and onion into a suitable small bowl. Cover and microwave on 100%/HIGH for 2 minutes.
2. Layer the ingredients into a medium-sized casserole, seasoning each layer with oregano, salt and pepper. Start

with potato, then liver, tomatoes, bacon and onion, and finish with a layer of potato.

3. Pour over the stock. Cover the dish and microwave on 70%/ROAST for 30 minutes, or until potatoes are cooked. Allow to stand for 10 minutes.
4. Brush potatoes with a little oil. Sprinkle with paprika and brown under the grill.

Traditionally, hot pots were really a stew with a topping of sliced potatoes (Lancashire Hot Pot). The lid was always removed for the last half-hour of the cooking time so that the potatoes could crisp and brown. This is why I suggest putting the cooked dish under the grill.

BEEF IN BEER

Lean beef and beer are a flavourful and warming combination. Canned red kidney beans are added to the casserole before serving, as the pulses are an excellent way of filling out the dish, which uses only a little high-fat meat. Serve with wholemeal French bread and a tossed green salad.

PREPARATION TIME: 20 minutes
MICROWAVE COOKING TIME: 1 hour 34 minutes
SERVES: 4

675 g (1½ lb) lean stewing beef, cubed
1 rounded tbsp flour
1 tsp dry mustard
1 tbsp corn oil
2 medium onions, chopped
1 carrot, peeled and sliced
1 courgette, sliced
1 tsp dried oregano
2 cloves garlic, crushed
140 ml (5 fl oz) beer
140 ml (5 fl oz) beef stock, hot
freshly ground black pepper
432 g (15 oz) can red kidney beans, drained

1. Toss the meat in the flour and mustard to coat.
2. Put the oil into a large casserole and microwave, uncovered, on 100%/HIGH for 1 minute.
3. Stir in the onions, carrot and courgette.
4. Cover and microwave on 100%/HIGH for 5 minutes. Stir.
5. Add the meat, cover and microwave on 100%/HIGH for 5 minutes. Add the oregano and garlic.
6. Pour over the beer and stock. Season with black pepper.
7. Cover and microwave on 100%/HIGH for 7 minutes.
8. Stir. Re-cover and microwave on 40%/SIMMER for 1 hour 15 minutes. Stir and re-cover twice during cooking.
9. Allow to stand, covered, for 10 minutes.
10. Stir in drained red kidney beans. Microwave for 2 minutes on 100%/HIGH. Serve immediately.

NOTE: This casserole improves a little if cooked in the morning and re-heated to serve. To re-heat, put the covered casserole into the microwave for 10–12 minutes on 100%/HIGH. Stir once after 7 minutes and again before serving.

Many people think it is impossible to achieve a really tender casserole of beef from the microwave oven. I believe they simply do not cook it on a low power for long enough. Just like cooking conventionally, the meat must be simmered gently until tender. Simply taste the meat at the end of cooking time. If the meat is not tender, return it for a further 15–20 minutes on 30%/DEFROST, then taste again. The result is every bit as good as a beef casserole cooked conventionally.

PORK WITH GINGER AND CABBAGE

Prunes were often used to flavour poultry and game recipes, and it was usual to mix different meats in the same recipe, e.g. beef with belly of pork, or chicken with pork. I have devised a recipe that uses a breast of chicken with pork fillet. The flavour of the finished dish is very good. Serve with rice.

PREPARATION TIME: 30 minutes
MICROWAVE COOKING TIME: 1 hour 4 minutes
SERVES: 3

2 tbsp corn oil
1 medium onion, sliced
1 stick celery, chopped
1 courgette, cut into matchsticks
225 g (8 oz) white cabbage, shredded
340 g (12 oz) pork fillet, diced
8 no-need-to-soak prunes
1 boneless chicken breast about 170 g (6 oz) in weight, diced
½ tsp ground ginger
170 ml (6 fl oz) medium dry white wine
freshly ground black pepper
1 sachet bouquet garni
2 tsp cornflour

TO SERVE
freshly chopped parsley

1. Put the oil into a large casserole. Microwave, uncovered, on 100%/HIGH for 1 minute. Stir in the prepared onion, celery, courgette and the white cabbage.
2. Cover and microwave on 100%/HIGH for 5 minutes. Stir.
3. Add the pork, the prunes and the chicken breast.
4. Sprinkle over the ginger. Pour over the wine. Season with black pepper and add the bouquet garni.
5. Cover and microwave on 100%/HIGH for 5 minutes. Stir, re-cover and microwave on 40%/SIMMER for 50 minutes, stirring and re-covering after 15 minutes.
6. Cream the cornflour to a smooth paste with a little water and stir into the casserole.
7. Microwave, uncovered, on 100%/HIGH for 2–3 minutes.
8. Allow to stand for 10 minutes, then stir and serve sprinkled with plenty of chopped parsley. Accompany with some cooked rice.

CHEESE, ONION AND PARSLEY PUDDING

Much lighter than the traditional steak and kidney pudding, this main-course dish is quick to prepare and cook. The flavour is excellent and the texture better than any savoury pud I have ever made conventionally. Serve with a freshly made tomato and onion sauce.

PREPARATION TIME: 15 minutes
MICROWAVE COOKING TIME: 9–12 minutes
SERVES: 4

1 medium onion, finely chopped
225 g (8 oz) self-raising flour
½ tsp salt
1 tsp baking powder
115 g (4 oz) shredded suet or hard margarine, chilled and grated
1 tsp dried parsley
115 g (4 oz) grated Cheddar cheese
about 200 ml (7 fl oz) milk and water, mixed

1. Put the chopped onion into a medium-sized bowl. Cover and microwave on 100%/HIGH for 2–3 minutes. Stir and set aside, uncovered, to cool a little.
2. Sift flour, salt and baking powder into a bowl.
3. Add the suet or margarine, parsley and Cheddar cheese. Mix well with a fork.
4. Fork in the onion.
5. Mix to a soft dough with the milk and water.
6. Lightly grease an 850 ml (1½ pt) boilable plastic pudding basin and fill with the dough.
7. Cover and microwave on 70%/ROAST for 7–9 minutes.
8. Allow to stand for 5 minutes, then turn out on to a serving dish and serve with tomato and onion sauce.

Since savoury puddings are now strongly associated with traditional British cooking, it is strange to discover that steak and kidney pudding was not actually recorded as a recipe until the nineteenth century.

Kent was well known for the fact that the people there enjoyed making puddings out of almost anything, so maybe our ancestors would not have been too surprised by my cheese, onion and parsley pudding, as I am a woman of Kent!

CHICKEN LIVERS WITH NEW POTATOES

Tiny new potatoes are cooked in the microwave with mint. While they stand, cook the chicken livers with onion, bacon and garlic. Coat the drained potatoes with the liver mixture and serve immediately, sprinkled with plenty of chopped parsley.

PREPARATION TIME: 15 minutes
MICROWAVE COOKING TIME: 19 minutes
SERVES: 4

450 g (1 lb) tiny new potatoes, scrubbed clean
sprig of fresh mint

FOR THE TOPPING
2 rashers unsmoked collar bacon, rind removed, chopped
1 medium onion, chopped
55 g (2 oz) polyunsaturated margarine
1 clove garlic, chopped
450 g (1 lb) chicken livers, roughly chopped
1 tbsp sherry

TO SERVE
plenty of finely chopped parsley

1. Put the scrubbed new potatoes into a 1.7 l (3 pt) casserole.
2. Pierce each potato once with a sharp knife to allow steam to escape. Add 2 tbsp water with a sprig of mint.
3. Cover and microwave on 100%/HIGH for 8 minutes. Set aside to stand, covered.
4. Prepare the sauce. Put the bacon, onion, margarine and garlic into another 1.7 l (3 pt) casserole. Cover and microwave on 100%/HIGH for 4 minutes. Stir.
5. Stir in the chicken livers. Cover and microwave on 100%/HIGH for 7 minutes, stirring and re-covering after 3 minutes.
6. Stir in the sherry.
7. Drain potatoes and turn on to warmed serving dish.
8. Top with the chicken liver mixture and serve immediately, sprinkled with plenty of chopped parsley.

SHEPHERD'S PIE

Traditionally made from meat left over from a joint, shepherd's pie is often high in fat and sadly lacking in flavour. Try this healthy version, which uses minced, filleted leg of lamb cooked in stock. The potato topping is brushed with egg yolk and browned under a pre-heated grill. Serve with minted peas.

PREPARATION TIME: 25 minutes
MICROWAVE COOKING TIME: 45 minutes
SERVES: 4

900 g (2 lb) white potatoes, peeled and diced
5 tbsp semi-skimmed milk
450 g (1 lb) filleted leg of lamb, minced
1 stick celery, chopped
1 small onion, chopped
1 tbsp flour
salt and freshly ground black pepper
2 tbsp tomato purée
2 tbsp red Bon (concentrated wine)
140 ml (¼ pt) well-flavoured stock

TO ADD TO THE POTATO TOPPING
2 tbsp cottage cheese
1 tbsp dried chives
½ tsp paprika
1 egg yolk

1. Put the potatoes into a medium-sized mixing bowl. Add 3 tbsp milk. Cover and microwave on 100%/HIGH for 15 minutes. Stir and set aside, covered.
2. Put the minced lamb, the celery and the onion into a casserole. Microwave, uncovered, on 100%/HIGH for 10 minutes, stirring every 3 minutes.
3. Stir in the flour. Season. Stir in the tomato purée, the Bon and the beef stock. Cover and microwave on 100%/HIGH for 4 minutes. Stir, re-cover and microwave on 40%/SIMMER for 12 minutes. Stir and turn into serving dish.
4. Pop the cooked potatoes back into the microwave on 100%/

HIGH for 2 minutes to re-heat, then mash down with a fork. Add the remaining milk with the cottage cheese.

5. Beat the potato until well creamed, beat in the chives and paprika, then spoon it over the meat base. Fork up to give a rough appearance.
6. Brush the surface of the potato all over with egg yolk.
7. Return the completed pie to the microwave for 2 minutes on 100%/HIGH, then brown under a pre-heated grill.
8. Serve immediately with the minted peas.

Shepherd's pie was a Victorian 'standby'. It was made using fresh or left-over cooked meat and the potatoes were mashed down and then creamed with plenty of butter and cream or full-fat milk. This low-fat version is no less tasty than the original dish, yet it is much healthier.

BRAISED PORK

Roast pork with apple sauce is often served as the traditional British Sunday lunch. Try this microwave recipe, which cooks this lean cut to perfection. Thicken the cooking liquid with cornflour to make a delicious gravy.

PREPARATION TIME: 15 minutes
MICROWAVE COOKING TIME: 1 hour 18 minutes
SERVES: 4–6

2 sticks celery, chopped
1 turnip, peeled and diced
12 small onions, halved
2 carrots, peeled and diced
1 bouquet garni
140 ml (¼ pt) cider or pure apple juice
1.5 kg (3½ lb) neck-end top joint of pork

1. Put all prepared vegetables into a suitable oblong casserole. Add 3 tbsp water. Cover and microwave on 100%/HIGH for 6 minutes.

2. Add the bouquet garni to the vegetables and stand the pork on top. Pour over the cider or apple juice.
3. Cover with a lid and microwave on 100%/HIGH for 12 minutes. Turn the joint over and re-cover.
4. Microwave on 40%/SIMMER for 1 hour.
5. Allow to stand for 15–20 minutes before carving.

Braising and oven-roasting in a closed oven became common only after the kitchen range became widely available in the nineteenth century. Before this, braising was carried out in a pot hung over a huge pot of boiling water. Roasting was done on a spit over an open fire.

BACON-AND-WALNUT-STUFFED CHICKEN

Fresh corn-fed chicken stuffed with a mixture of bacon, brown breadcrumbs and walnuts, then roasted on a rack. The walnuts give a lovely flavour to the bird.

PREPARATION TIME: 25 minutes
MICROWAVE COOKING TIME: about 30 minutes
SERVES: 6

1.8 kg (4 lb) fresh roasting chicken
45 g (1½ oz) polyunsaturated margarine

FOR THE STUFFING
85 g (3 oz) shelled walnuts, finely chopped
55 g (2 oz) fresh brown breadcrumbs
2 rashers lean streaky bacon, de-rinded and chopped
½ tsp dried sage
salt and freshly ground black pepper
1 egg, size 4, beaten

TO COAT THE CHICKEN
2–3 tsp paprika pepper
½ tsp casserole seasoning

1. Put the breadcrumbs, walnuts, chopped bacon and sage into a mixing bowl. Season with a little salt and some freshly ground pepper. Bind together with the beaten egg.
2. Spoon the stuffing into the neck end of the bird, taking care not to pack too tightly. Secure with wooden cocktail sticks.
3. Put the margarine into a small bowl and microwave on 70%/ROAST for 1 minute, or until melted.
4. Using a pastry brush, brush the melted margarine all over the bird.
5. Combine the paprika and casserole seasoning and sprinkle all over the bird.
6. Weigh the prepared bird and calculate cooking time, allowing 7 minutes per 450 g (1 lb) in a 700 W oven.
7. Arrange the bird on a microwave meat-roasting rack, or on an upturned tea-plate in a suitable shallow dish.
8. Cover with a split microwave roasting bag, keeping the bag inside the rim of the dish. Do not use tin foil (see p. 15).
9. Microwave on 100%/HIGH for calculated cooking time.
10. Allow to stand, covered with a sheet of foil, for 15 minutes before serving.

Freshly killed poultry figured widely in the national diet of our forefathers. The flavour and texture was far superior to the intensively reared and almost always frozen birds we buy today. However, correctly defrosted and carefully cooked poultry can still taste very good, and the microwave does improve the flavour of chicken. This recipe does use a fresh chicken, but, if necessary, a defrosted frozen bird may be used. Although chickens can be successfully defrosted in the microwave, I prefer a bird that has been slowly defrosted in the fridge.

TURKEY BREASTS IN TOMATO SAUCE

Lean turkey breasts are an ideal high-protein, low-fat food. Cook with tomatoes, onions and leeks and decorate with sprigs of watercress. This dish is ideal for entertaining and a meal that will be welcomed by any weight-watcher.

PREPARATION TIME: 15 minutes
MICROWAVE COOKING TIME: 23 minutes
SERVES: 4

4 turkey breasts, about 170 g (6 oz) each, defrosted if frozen

FOR THE SAUCE
2 onions, peeled and finely chopped
2 cloves garlic, crushed
3 rashers streaky bacon, de-rinded and chopped
115 g (4 oz) button mushrooms, sliced
3 large finger carrots, peeled and sliced
1 tsp dried thyme
1 tbsp Worcestershire sauce
400 g (14 oz) can chopped tomatoes
2 tbsp tomato purée
salt and freshly ground black pepper

TO GARNISH
sprigs of fresh watercress

1. Lay the turkey breasts in a single layer in a fairly shallow dish.
2. Prepare the sauce. Put the onions, garlic, bacon, mushrooms, carrots and thyme into a medium-sized casserole. Add 2 tbsp water. Cover with a lid and microwave on 100%/HIGH for 5 minutes. Stir.
3. Stir the Worcestershire sauce, tomatoes and tomato purée into the partly cooked vegetables. Season with salt and pepper.
4. Pour the sauce over the turkey breasts.
5. Cover and microwave on 100%/HIGH for 3 minutes, then continue to microwave on 50%/MEDIUM for 15 minutes, or until the turkey is cooked.
6. Allow to stand, covered, for 5 minutes, then serve garnished with the sprigs of watercress.

Turkey breasts are now widely available frozen and turkey is a wonderful healthy food, which takes on a delicious flavour if cooked with garlic and tomatoes.

CHICKEN BREASTS IN CHEESE SAUCE

Use reduced-fat Cheddar cheese in the sauce and top with Parmesan cheese before grilling. The garlic and cheese combine well with the celery and onion to make a delicious supper dish. Serve with some freshly cooked broccoli and rice.

PREPARATION TIME: 20 minutes
MICROWAVE COOKING TIME: 17 minutes
SERVES: 4

30 g (1 oz) butter
4 boneless chicken breasts abut 170 g (6 oz) each
1 medium onion, chopped
2 cloves garlic, crushed
410 g (14½ oz) can celery hearts, drained and sliced
salt and freshly ground black pepper
285 ml (½ pt) pouring cheese sauce, warm
2 tbsp grated Parmesan cheese

1. Melt the butter in a dish in the microwave on 70%/ROAST for 1 minute, or until melted. Arrange the chicken breasts in a single layer in a shallow dish. Brush all over with the melted butter.
2. Cover and microwave on 100%/HIGH for 4 minutes. Turn each chicken breast over. Re-cover and continue to microwave on 100%/HIGH for 4 minutes. Set aside.
3. Put the onion into a serving dish. Cover and microwave on 100%/HIGH for 3 minutes. Stir. Add garlic and the sliced celery hearts.
4. Arrange the chicken breasts on top of the vegetables. Season with salt and pepper.
5. Pour the cheese sauce over the chicken to coat evenly and sprinkle with Parmesan.
6. Microwave, uncovered, on 50%/MEDIUM for about 6 minutes, or until heated through.
7. Brown under a pre-heated grill, then serve immediately with broccoli and rice.

LAMB CURRY

The meat is supplemented by lentils, fruit and vegetables to make a filling curry. Serve with brown rice. A healthy traditional meal.

PREPARATION TIME: 30 minutes
MICROWAVE COOKING TIME: 37 minutes
SERVES: 4

1 medium onion, chopped
1 clove garlic, chopped
1 large carrot, peeled and chopped
1 courgette, sliced
85 g (3 oz) red lentils
1 rounded tbsp plain flour
1 tsp hot Madras curry powder
½ tsp allspice
675 g (1 lb 8 oz) lean filleted leg of lamb, minced
30 g (1 oz) dried apricots, chopped
425 ml (¾ pt) vegetable stock, hot
3 rings canned pineapple in natural juice, chopped

TO SERVE
plenty of finely chopped parsley

1. Put the prepared onion, garlic, carrot and courgette into a large casserole.
2. Cover and microwave on 100%/HIGH for 5 minutes, stirring and re-covering after 3 minutes.
3. Add the lentils.
4. Combine the flour, curry powder and allspice in a plastic bag. Add the lamb and toss to coat. Add to casserole with the dried apricots. Pour over the stock. Stir well.
5. Cover and microwave on 70%/ROAST for 30 minutes, stirring and re-covering three times during cooking.
6. Stir in the chopped pineapple pieces. Return to microwave for 1–2 minutes on 100%/HIGH to re-heat.
7. Serve immediately, sprinkled with plenty of finely chopped parsley.

LAMBS' LIVER WITH VEGETABLES

Liver provides a good supply of iron. Protein, vitamin A and the vitamin B complex are also present. In traditional British recipes liver was often 'boiled until firm' as quoted in Mrs Beeton's *All About Cookery*. However, we now know that calves' liver and lambs' liver in particular are best cooked quickly and served slightly pink in the centre. This microwave recipe cooks liver to perfection, and the finished dish is presented on a colourful array of vegetables with a parsley sauce. Mashed potatoes make a good accompaniment.

PREPARATION TIME: 15 minutes
MICROWAVE COOKING TIME: 23 minutes
SERVES: 3

450 g (1 lb) leeks, cleaned and sliced
115 g (4 oz) broccoli spears, florets only
285 g (10 oz) finger carrots, sliced
340 g (12 oz) lambs' liver
30 g (1 oz) vegetable margarine
2 rashers back bacon, de-rinded and cut into strips

FOR THE SAUCE
30 g (1 oz) vegetable margarine
30 g (1 oz) flour
salt and freshly ground black pepper
285 ml (½ pt) vegetable stock or semi-skimmed milk
1 tbsp finely chopped fresh parsley

1. Put all the prepared vegetables into a medium-sized casserole. Add 2 tbsp water.
2. Cover and microwave on 100%/HIGH for 10 minutes, stirring and re-covering after 5 minutes. Set aside, covered.
3. Cut the liver into thin strips. Put the margarine into a shallow dish and microwave, uncovered, on 100%/HIGH for 30 seconds – 1 minute, or until melted and hot.
4. Stir the slices of liver and bacon into the melted margarine.
5. Cover and microwave on 70%/ROAST for 4–5 minutes, stirring and re-covering after 2 minutes. Set aside, covered.

6. Make the sauce. Put the margarine into a litre (2 pt) jug and microwave on 100%/HIGH for 45 seconds, or until melted and hot. Stir in the flour. Season. Gradually add the stock or milk, stirring all the time.
7. Microwave, uncovered, on 100%/HIGH for 3–4 minutes, stirring frequently with a balloon whisk. The sauce must rise in the jug and thicken.
8. Beat in any juices from the liver and from the vegetables.
9. Fold in the parsley.
10. Lift the cooked liver slices on to the cooked vegetables and pour over the sauce.
11. Return the dish to the microwave and re-heat for 2–3 minutes on 100%/HIGH. Serve immediately.

Liver 'n' onions has always been a traditional standby. Liver was cooked with plenty of onions to try and disguise its very strong flavour. If children find the flavour of liver a bit strong, lay it out in a shallow dish, cover with milk and allow to stand for half an hour, then drain and pat dry on kitchen paper before continuing with the recipe.

MEAT LOAF RING

Lean minced beef combines well with part-cooked vegetables to produce a colourful meat loaf, which cooks well in the microwave and looks even more attractive if cooked in a ring mould. This versatile dish may be served hot or cold, and I like to fill the centre with something appropriate – a salad garnish if serving the ring cold, or freshly cooked new potatoes and carrots sprinkled with parsley if serving hot. A freshly made tomato sauce accompanies the dish well.

PREPARATION TIME: 20 minutes
MICROWAVE COOKING TIME: 15 minutes
SERVES: 6

1 onion, chopped
2 carrots, peeled and chopped
450 g (1 lb) lean chuck steak, minced
225 g (8 oz) pork sausage-meat
55 g (2 oz) fresh brown breadcrumbs
1 Cox's apple, chopped
1 tsp dried sage
1 tsp made English mustard
1 tbsp tomato sauce
freshly ground black pepper
a little beaten egg to bind

1. Put the onion and carrots in a medium-sized bowl or casserole. Add 1 tbsp water.
2. Cover and microwave on 100%/HIGH for 3 minutes. Stir.
3. Put the minced beef and the sausage-meat into a large mixing bowl with the breadcrumbs. Work with the hands to combine.
4. Add the part-cooked vegetables, the apple, the sage, the mustard and the tomato sauce. Season with pepper.
5. Add enough beaten egg to bind the mixture together.
6. Press the mixture into a 23 cm (9″) re-usable microwave ring mould.
7. Microwave on 70%/ROAST for 10–12 minutes.
8. Remove from microwave and pour off and discard any excess fat.
9. Serve immediately if serving hot, or allow to cool in ring mould, then turn out and garnish, if serving cold.

NOTE: To make this loaf look more appealing it may be glazed while still warm with a 'browning agent'. Simply mix half a teaspoon of concentrated beef stock, such as Bovril, with 1 tbsp tomato sauce and, using a pastry brush, brush the loaf all over.

KEDGEREE

Although originally brought from India, kedgeree soon became a popular breakfast dish in this country. We are now far more inclined to serve this nutritious, low-fat dish for lunch or supper. Vary the recipe by using different fish. Serve with bread rolls and a mixed salad.

PREPARATION TIME: 10 minutes
MICROWAVE COOKING TIME: 17 minutes
SERVES: 4

2 tbsp vegetable oil
2 medium onions, cut into rings
170 g (6 oz) long-grain rice
1 tsp medium-hot curry powder
565 ml (1 pt) chicken stock, boiling
450 g (1 lb) finnan haddock
2 tbsp semi-skimmed milk
3 hard-boiled eggs, peeled and chopped
1 tbsp finely chopped parsley

1. Heat the oil conventionally in a shallow frying-pan. Gently fry the onions in the hot oil until crisp and golden. Drain on kitchen paper. Set aside and keep warm.
2. Meanwhile rinse the rice with cold water, then drain and place in a really large casserole or mixing bowl. Add the curry powder.
3. Pour on the boiling stock. Cover and microwave on 100%/HIGH for 9 minutes. Set aside, covered, for 7 minutes.
4. Arrange the haddock in a single layer in a shallow dish. Pour over the milk. Cover and microwave on 100%/HIGH for 5–6 minutes, or until the fish flakes easily.
5. Fluff up the rice, mixing in the onion rings, hard-boiled eggs and parsley. Add the flaked fish, discarding any bones.
6. Cover the bowl or casserole and microwave on 100%/HIGH for 2 minutes, then turn into a serving dish and serve immediately, accompanied by bread rolls and a mixed salad.

VEGETARIAN RICE

Brown rice is cooked in the microwave with garlic and onion, then combined with mixed vegetables, walnuts, pine nuts and cubed blue cheese. Serve warm or cold with a green salad comprising Iceberg lettuce, cucumber, celery and sliced Cox's apple.

PREPARATION TIME: 12 minutes
MICROWAVE COOKING TIME: 27 minutes
SERVES: 4

1 clove garlic, crushed
1 medium onion, chopped
30 g (1 oz) butter
1 red pepper, chopped
225 g (8 oz) Uncle Ben's whole-grain rice
565 ml (1 pt) vegetable stock, boiling
200 g (8 oz) frozen mixed vegetables, peas, beans, sweetcorn, carrots
55 g (2 oz) toasted pine nuts
55 g (2 oz) chopped walnuts
115 g (4 oz) blue cheese, diced

TO SERVE
freshly chopped parsley

1. Put the garlic, onion, butter and red pepper into a 3.4 l (6 pt) casserole. Cover with a lid and microwave on 100%/HIGH for 2 minutes.
2. Add rice and stock. Cover and microwave on 100%/HIGH for 20 minutes.
3. Allow to stand, covered, for 10 minutes.
4. Meanwhile put the frozen mixed vegetables into a medium-sized casserole. Cover and microwave on 100%/HIGH for 5 minutes, stirring and re-covering after 3 minutes.
5. After the rice has stood, remove the lid and fork up the rice, adding the drained mixed vegetables, the toasted pine nuts, the chopped walnuts and the diced blue cheese.
6. Serve warm or cold, topped with plenty of freshly chopped parsley.

NOTE: If serving cold, it is better to add the diced cheese and the nuts once the rice and vegetables have cooled.

TOMATOES WITH MONKFISH

Monkfish is often known as poor man's scampi. It combines well with tomatoes to make a wonderful supper dish. Serve with plain boiled potatoes, rice or pasta.

PREPARATION TIME: 20 minutes
MICROWAVE COOKING TIME: 16 minutes
SERVES: 4

900 g (2 lb) monkfish
450 g (1 lb) ripe tomatoes
1 tbsp oil
1 green pepper, de-seeded and chopped
1 medium onion, chopped
1 clove garlic, crushed
1 tbsp flour, rounded
salt and freshly ground black pepper
1 tbsp tomato purée
70 ml (2.5 fl oz) dry white wine

TO SERVE
2 level tbsp finely chopped parsley

1. Skin the monkfish, then remove the flesh from the bone. Cut into 2.5 cm (1″) chunks.
2. Peel and chop tomatoes, discarding pips.
3. Put the oil into a large, shallow dish and microwave for 1 minute on 100%/HIGH.
4. Stir the green pepper, the crushed garlic and the onion into the oil. Cover and microwave on 100%/HIGH for 3 minutes. Stir in the flour and microwave on 100%/HIGH for 1 minute.
5. Season lightly, then add the tomato purée, the chopped tomatoes and the wine. Stir well. Microwave on 100%/HIGH for 3 minutes. Stir every minute.

6. Stir in the prepared fish. Cover and microwave on 100%/HIGH for 6–8 minutes, stirring twice, or until fish flakes easily.
7. Serve sprinkled with the chopped parsley.

Vegetables, Salads and Fish Dishes

Vegetables prepared in a variety of ways produce wonderful side dishes, be they served hot or cold. Many of these recipes combine vegetables with other ingredients and so extend them into main meals. High in fibre and therefore sustaining, many fruits and vegetables are readily available fresh or frozen. As the microwave oven enables vegetables and fruit to be cooked in the very minimum of liquid, all the colour, flavour and most of the nutrients remain in the food, instead of being drained into the cooking liquid. Use these recipes to encourage people to try vegetables in different ways.

The fish caught off our shores is still vastly under-used on our tables. Fish is an almost perfect food, high in protein and calcium, and white fish in particular is very low in fat, while oily fish has dispersed through its tissue polyunsaturated fat, which is the kind of fat conducive to a healthy heart. The microwave will deal speedily with fresh fish, leaving few lingering smells to taint the kitchen. Remember also that fish may be microwaved straight from frozen on 100%/HIGH if required, or use your DEFROST control first and then go on to cook the defrosted fish after a short standing time. Due to the fat content of oily fish it is obviously higher in calories than white fish and therefore more sustaining, leaving us feeling fuller for a little longer.

MIXED VEGETABLE AND BEAN CASSEROLE

Pulses are a cheap source of protein. They also supply carbohydrate, thiamin, iron and calcium. A high-fibre vegetable casserole, which is ideal for vegetarians.

PREPARATION TIME: 20 minutes
MICROWAVE COOKING TIME: 30 minutes
SERVES: 4–6

140 g (5 oz) five-bean mix, cooked (see note)
450 g (1 lb) potatoes, scrubbed clean and diced
2 medium onions, chopped

2 medium carrots, peeled and sliced
2 medium leeks, cleaned and sliced
1 medium courgette, sliced
85 g (3 oz) frozen peas, defrosted
freshly ground black pepper
565 ml (1 pt) vegetable stock, hot
3 tbsp semi-skimmed milk
85 g (3 oz) vegetarian Cheddar cheese

1. Choose a large casserole, about 2.3 l (4 pt) in capacity.
2. Arrange the vegetables and cooked beans in layers, seasoning each layer with black pepper. Add the milk.
3. Pour over the stock. Cover with a lid and microwave for about 30 minutes on 100%/HIGH, or until vegetables are tender. Stir in peas. Set aside, covered, for 10 minutes, then remove lid and sprinkle with the grated cheese. Serve either immediately, or (if you have used a suitable casserole) after browning the cheese topping under the grill.

NOTE: To cook 140 g (5 oz) five-bean mix in the microwave, soak for at least 6 hours, overnight if preferred. Drain. Cover with boiling water. Cover with a lid and microwave on 100%/HIGH for 10 minutes, then continue to microwave on 40%/SIMMER for about 20 minutes, or until beans are tender. Set aside for 5 minutes, then drain, and the beans are ready to be used in this recipe.

Beans were frequently used by the poor to thicken soups and stews.

COURGETTES WITH BACON AND ORANGE

A simple side dish. The bacon is cooked on a rack or on absorbent kitchen paper so that much of the fat is removed as the bacon crisps.

PREPARATION TIME: 15 minutes
MICROWAVE COOKING TIME: 12–15 minutes
SERVES: 4

675 g (1½ lb) courgettes, topped, tailed and sliced
4 medium tomatoes, skinned and chopped
½ tsp celery seasoning
rind and juice of ½ an orange
4 rashers streaky bacon, de-rinded
1 rounded tsp cornflour

1. Put the courgettes into a medium-sized casserole.
2. Add the tomatoes, celery seasoning and the orange rind and juice.
3. Cover and microwave on 100%/HIGH for 7–9 minutes, stirring and re-covering once, halfway through cooking time. Set aside.
4. Arrange the bacon in a single layer on a microwave roasting rack or on two sheets of good quality absorbent kitchen paper, arranged on a dinner plate. Cover with a sheet of kitchen paper in both cases.
5. Microwave on 100%/HIGH for 3–4 minutes, or until bacon is crisp. Allow to stand for 2 minutes.
6. Meanwhile mix cornflour to a smooth paste with a little water and stir into courgette mixture. Microwave, uncovered, on 100%/HIGH for 2 minutes. Stir well.
7. Serve the courgettes sprinkled with the chopped bacon – I simply snip it with scissors.

MASHED POTATOES WITH WATERCRESS

A good source of vitamin C, no meal could be easier to microwave or more popular, particularly with youngsters, than good old mashed potatoes. Watercress adds vitamins A and C and iron and calcium. The spring onion adds flavour.

PREPARATION TIME: 15 minutes
MICROWAVE COOKING TIME: 12 minutes
SERVES: 4

675 g (1½ lb) old potatoes, peeled and diced
3 tbsp semi-skimmed milk
2 tbsp soured cream
2 spring onions, chopped
½ bunch fresh watercress, chopped

1. Put the diced potatoes into a large casserole. Add the milk. Cover with a lid and microwave on 100%/HIGH for 12 minutes, stirring once halfway through cooking time. Set aside, covered, for 6 minutes.
2. Mash down the potatoes and milk and add the soured cream. Fluff up. Add a little extra milk if necessary.
3. Fold in the chopped spring onions and watercress.
4. Serve immediately.

Potatoes eventually replaced globe artichokes as the staple diet for the poor and were frequently served, in some form, three times a day. Now it is often difficult to obtain a good choice of types of potato from the greengrocer. There are so many varieties of the humble potato, it is a great shame that we do not demand a better choice and a higher standard.

POTATO AND CHIVE SALAD

The humble potato contains carbohydrate and a little protein, and as we British eat potatoes in quantity, the vitamin C content is significant, too. The light yoghurt dressing is poured over the potatoes while they are still warm.

PREPARATION TIME: 10 minutes
MICROWAVE COOKING TIME: 10 minutes
SERVES: 4

675 g (1½ lb) new potatoes, scrubbed clean, diced

FOR THE DRESSING

3 tbsp natural set yoghurt
85 ml (3 fl oz) soured cream
1 tbsp semi-skimmed milk
a few chopped chives
a little seasoning (optional)

1. Put the diced potatoes into a large casserole. Add 2 tbsp water. Cover and microwave on 100%/HIGH for 10 minutes. Stir and re-cover after 5 minutes. Set aside, covered.
2. To prepare the dressing, combine the yoghurt with the soured cream and semi-skimmed milk. Fold in the chives and season if required.
3. Drain the potatoes and turn into serving dish. Top with the dressing and serve immediately.

NOTE: The dressing on its own, made up without the milk, makes a refreshing dip for parties.

FENNEL WITH CELERY AND TOMATO

Fennel was grown in most English gardens in the seventeenth century, and was widely used in cookery. Unfortunately it is now fairly rare to find fennel in a British kitchen garden.

Florentine fennel is widely available in this country. It has a mild aniseed flavour and is delicious served hot or cold. This recipe provides fibre and vitamin C.

PREPARATION TIME: 15 minutes
MICROWAVE COOKING TIME: 10 minutes
SERVES: 4

1 large or 2 small bulbs fennel
1 large onion, finely chopped
4 sticks celery, chopped
2 cloves garlic, crushed
400 g (14 oz) can chopped tomatoes
salt and freshly ground black pepper
30 g (1 oz) freshly grated Cheddar cheese
55 g (2 oz) flaked almonds, toasted (see p. 49)

1. Cut away coarse outer leaves from fennel and discard the root base. Cut off the feathery tops and keep to use as a garnish. Slice the bulbs very thinly.
2. Layer the fennel slices and chopped onion into a large casserole with the chopped celery and the crushed garlic.
3. Pour over the tomatoes, then season with a little salt and pepper.
4. Cover and microwave on 100%/HIGH for 10 minutes, or until vegetables are cooked to your liking. Stir and re-cover once during cooking.
5. Set aside for 5 minutes, then sprinkle with the cheese and almonds and serve immediately.

NOTE: If you prefer not to use the cheese and almond topping, the vegetables may be served topped with a few snipped chives.

MANGE-TOUT WITH BEANSPROUTS AND MUSHROOMS

A hot vegetable dish, which is full of colour and flavour. Mushrooms contain vitamin B, and the mange-tout provides some protein. Serve with wholemeal scones and vegetable pâté.

PREPARATION TIME: 10 minutes
MICROWAVE COOKING TIME: 13½ minutes
SERVES: 4–6

4 tbsp sunflower oil
1 medium onion, finely chopped
340 g (12 oz) beansprouts
450 g (1 lb) fresh or frozen mange-tout
2 tbsp soya sauce
225 g (8 oz) button mushrooms, sliced
1 orange, peeled and divided into segments

1. Put 2 tbsp sunflower oil into a large casserole. Microwave, uncovered, on 100%/HIGH for 1 minute.

2. Add the onion. Stir well.
3. Cover and microwave on 100%/HIGH for 2 minutes. Stir in the beansprouts and the mange-tout with the soya sauce. Cover and microwave on 100%/HIGH for 10 minutes, stirring and re-covering after 5 minutes. Allow to stand for 3 minutes. Transfer vegetables to serving dish, using slotted spoon.
4. Meanwhile heat the remaining oil in a frying-pan on your conventional cooker and stir-fry the mushrooms until crisp. Drain on absorbent kitchen paper.
5. Serve the beansprout stir-fry topped with the crisp mushrooms and garnished with the segments of orange.
6. Hand warm wholemeal scones and some vegetable pâté round separately.

ONION-AND-CHEESE-STUFFED MUSHROOMS

Serve two of these mushrooms per person as a main meal, or one as a snack or vegetable dish. Accompany with rice and salad.

Fibre, protein, carbohydrate, vitamins and fat are all provided in this nutritious dish. A recipe specially formulated for vegetarians.

PREPARATION TIME: 15 minutes
MICROWAVE COOKING TIME: 13 minutes
SERVES: 3–6

1 medium onion, finely chopped
6 large flat mushrooms
2 tbsp corn oil
85 g (3 oz) vegetable margarine
55 g (2 oz) wholemeal breadcrumbs, fresh
30 g (1 oz) quick-cooking oats
1 tsp dried parsley
½ tsp made mustard, English
115 g (4 oz) vegetarian Cheddar, grated
salt and freshly ground black pepper
1 egg, size 3, beaten

1. Put onion into cereal bowl. Cover and microwave for 2 minutes on 100%/HIGH.
2. Gently remove stalks from mushrooms. Chop stalks and set aside.
3. Brush mushrooms on both sides with oil and arrange three mushrooms on each of two dinner plates.
4. Put 55 g (2 oz) vegetable margarine into a large casserole and microwave, uncovered, on 100%/HIGH for 1 minute. Stir in the breadcrumbs and oats. Mix really well until margarine is evenly absorbed. Stir in cooked onion and chopped mushroom stalks.
5. Microwave, uncovered, for 2 minutes on 100%/HIGH. Stir. Microwave, uncovered, for a further 2 minutes. Stir and set aside for 5 minutes.
6. Add the dried parsley, the made mustard and 85 g (3 oz) of the grated cheese to the ingredients in the large casserole. Mix well. Season and add the beaten egg. Mix well again.
7. Divide the filling between the prepared mushrooms.
8. Divide remaining cheese between mushrooms, topping the filling evenly.
9. Cook each plate of three mushrooms, separately and uncovered, for 3 minutes on 100%/HIGH.
10. Serve immediately on a bed of rice, accompanied by a green salad.

NOTE: This recipe also makes a delicious starter. I serve one mushroom per person with a salad garnish and hand round some buttered brown or wholemeal bread separately.

POTATO AND BROAD BEAN SALAD

A filling, high-fibre salad in which the fruit and vegetables provide carbohydrate and Vitamin C. The yoghurt, mayonnaise and nuts add fat and protein.

Broad beans, potatoes and cabbage combined with English apples and nuts, tossed in mayonnaise and served on a bed of curly endive – a very English recipe.

PREPARATION TIME: 20 minutes
MICROWAVE COOKING TIME: 10 minutes
SERVES: 6

675 g (1½ lb) potatoes, scrubbed and diced evenly
225 g (8 oz) fresh white cabbage, shredded finely
1 Discovery apple, cored and chopped
1 Cox's apple, cored and chopped
55 g (2 oz) raisins
285 g (10 oz) can broad beans
3 tbsp reduced-calorie mayonnaise
2 tbsp natural yoghurt
a little milk
1 tsp tomato purée
salt and garlic pepper, if required
55 g (2 oz) roasted cashew nuts or shelled peanuts

TO SERVE
a bed of curly endive

1. Put the potatoes into a medium-sized casserole. Add 2 tbsp water. Cover and microwave on 100%/HIGH for 10 minutes, stirring gently and re-covering after 5 minutes. Set aside, covered, until cold.
2. Put the white cabbage into a large mixing bowl with the chopped apples and the raisins. Add cooled, drained potatoes and drained broad beans.
3. Mix together the mayonnaise, yoghurt, milk and tomato purée and pour over. Toss to coat, seasoning lightly if required.
4. Serve on a bed of curly endive, sprinkled with the roasted cashew nuts or shelled walnuts.

NOTE: The cashew nuts may be roasted in the microwave. Put cashew-nut kernels into a small casserole dish with 15 g (½ oz) vegetable margarine. Cook, uncovered, for about 3 minutes, stirring twice. Stand for 2 minutes, then drain on absorbent kitchen paper and serve.

Bulgur and Cashew Nut Salad

Bulgur, or cracked wheat, is a dried wheat product available from health-food stores. It is extremely economical and easy to use, yielding fibre and a little protein. It is used widely in the Middle East and may be used instead of rice in many of our traditional recipes. Serve with a mixed salad.

PREPARATION TIME: 10 minutes
MICROWAVE COOKING TIME: 3 minutes
SERVES: 4

225 g (8 oz) bulgur (cracked wheat)
1 large English onion, chopped
4 sticks celery, fairly finely chopped
1 carrot, peeled and grated
1 tsp mild curry powder
grated rind and juice of ½ orange
3 tomatoes, skinned and chopped
freshly ground black pepper
115 g (4 oz) lightly salted, roasted cashew nuts

1. Put the bulgur wheat into a bowl and cover with cold water. Set aside to soak for 15 minutes. Drain well and squeeze out as much water as possible – easiest done by putting the soaked bulgur in a sieve and squeezing moisture out with a wooden spoon.
2. Put the onion and celery into a large casserole. Cover with a lid and microwave on 100%/HIGH for 3 minutes, stirring and re-covering after 1 minute. Set aside to cool.
3. When cool, add to the softened vegetables the drained bulgur, the grated carrot, the curry powder, the rind and juice of the orange and the tomatoes. Mix well and season with the pepper.
4. Cover and set aside for half an hour for the flavours to mingle.
5. Add the cashew nuts just before serving.

SWEDE AND BROCCOLI LAYER

An attractive combination of colours and flavours. The vegetables should be cooked separately, but the dish may be cooked in the morning and re-heated when you are ready to serve it. Traditional vegetables at their best, served with a creamy sauce. Add a brown rice or pasta salad for a full vegetarian meal.

PREPARATION TIME: 30 minutes
MICROWAVE COOKING TIME: 32 minutes
SERVES: 4

450 g (1 lb) swede, peeled and diced
450 g (1 lb) broccoli, trimmed and cut into spears

FOR THE SAUCE
30 g (1 oz) vegetable margarine
45 g (1½ oz) plain flour
salt and freshly ground black pepper
340 ml (12 fl oz) semi-skimmed milk
115 g (4 oz) button mushrooms, finely chopped
2 slices wholemeal bread, toasted

1. Put the prepared swede into a large casserole dish. Add 2 tbsp cold water. Cover and microwave on 100%/HIGH for 12 minutes, stirring and re-covering after 6 minutes. Set aside.
2. Put the prepared broccoli into a large casserole. Add 3 tbsp cold water. Cover and microwave for 8–10 minutes, stirring and re-covering once during cooking. Set aside.
3. Put the margarine into a large 2.3 l (4 pt) mixing bowl. Microwave, uncovered, for 30 seconds – 1 minute on 100%/HIGH. Stir in flour and season lightly. Gradually blend in milk. Microwave, uncovered, for 5–6 minutes on 100%/HIGH, stirring frequently with a balloon whisk. The sauce must boil and thicken.
4. Drain swede and return to casserole. Drain broccoli and arrange evenly over swede.
5. Fold mushrooms into the hot sauce. (The mushrooms will cook quite sufficiently in the heat of the sauce.)

6. Pour sauce over cooked vegetables to coat evenly.
7. Cover and microwave on 100%/HIGH for about 3 minutes to re-heat.
8. Meanwhile toast the wholemeal bread and cut into triangles. Arrange attractively round edge of re-heated vegetable dish. Serve immediately accompanied by a brown rice or pasta salad.

Broccoli, as the name suggests, came to our shores from Italy. It was quickly adopted and became widely used. Today it is very much in vogue and readily available fresh and frozen.

BROWN RICE AND VEGETABLE SALAD

Brown rice, with its pleasant nutty flavour, is high in fibre and contains some protein. Combined with crisp vegetables and fruit, this healthy salad will prove popular with almost everyone.

PREPARATION TIME: 15 minutes
MICROWAVE COOKING TIME: 30 minutes
SERVES: 4

225 g (8 oz) long-grain brown rice, washed
700 ml (1¼ pt) well-flavoured vegetable stock, boiling
115 g (4 oz) dried apricots, chopped
1 courgette, grated
2 sticks celery, chopped
salt and freshly ground black pepper

FOR THE DRESSING
140 ml (5 fl oz) soured cream
1 tbsp freshly chopped mint
grated rind of ½ lemon
115 g (4 oz) salted peanuts

TO SERVE
Webb's Wonder lettuce, shredded

1. Put the brown rice into a large casserole. Pour over the boiling stock. Cover and microwave on 100%/HIGH for 30 minutes. Set aside, covered, for 10 minutes.
2. Gently fork up rice, adding the chopped apricots. Cover and set aside until cold.
3. Add the celery and courgettes. Season lightly.
4. Combine all ingredients for the dressing and mix with a fork. Pour over rice mixture. Toss to coat, then serve immediately on a bed of shredded lettuce, topped with the peanuts.

Brown rice is nutritionally better than white: as well as providing more fibre, it provides vitamin B, which is almost all removed from white rice. Rice in one form or another is the staple diet of more than half the human race.

RICE LAYER WITH MUSHROOMS

A delicious vegetable dish in which protein is provided by the peas, and the garlic adds flavour. Serve with a fresh tomato sauce and a mixed salad.

PREPARATION TIME: 10 minutes
MICROWAVE COOKING TIME: 35 minutes
SERVES: 4

1 medium onion, chopped
1 clove garlic, chopped
225 g (8 oz) brown rice
225 g (8 oz) frozen button mushrooms
565 ml (1 pt) well-flavoured vegetable stock, boiling
170 g (6 oz) frozen peas

1. Put the onion and garlic into a large casserole. Cover and microwave on 100%/HIGH for 2 minutes.
2. Stir in the rice with the mushrooms. Pour on the boiling stock.

3. Cover and microwave on 100%/HIGH for 30 minutes, without removing the lid.
4. Allow to stand for 5 minutes. Fork up.
5. Add frozen peas, cover and microwave on 100%/HIGH for 3 minutes. Serve immediately.

CREAMED SWEDE

Swede, sadly, seems to have gone out of fashion, maybe due to the time it takes to cook conventionally. It cooks a little quicker in the microwave and the flavour is superb, so do try this filling vegetable dish, which is creamy and delicious.

PREPARATION TIME: 10 minutes
MICROWAVE COOKING TIME: 35 minutes
SERVES: 4

2 cloves garlic, crushed
675 g (1½ lb) swede, peeled and diced
170 ml (7 fl oz) vegetable stock + 3 tbsp vegetable stock
½ tsp ground nutmeg
30 g (1 oz) butter
salt and freshly ground black pepper
142 ml (5 fl oz) carton soured cream
4 tbsp semi-skimmed milk
½ tsp dried parsley

1. Put the crushed garlic and the prepared swede into a medium-sized casserole. Season.
2. Add all but 3 tbsp of the stock, and the nutmeg.
3. Cover and microwave on 100%/HIGH for 25–30 minutes, stirring and re-covering twice during cooking. Set aside, covered, for 5 minutes, then turn contents of casserole into a food processor or liquidizer. Add remaining stock. Process until smooth.
4. Add the soured cream, butter and milk with the parsley and process again. Turn into casserole. Level surface.
5. Cover and microwave on 50%/MEDIUM for 5 minutes. Serve immediately.

Cabbage with Tomato and Apple

Cabbage is an excellent source of fibre and provides some vitamin C. Cooked with tomatoes and garlic, sweetened with raisins and an eating apple, this recipe is a good one to encourage those who have decided they don't like cabbage – often due to school-lunch memories of a steaming, smelly mass of overcooked greens!

PREPARATION TIME: 20 minutes
MICROWAVE COOKING TIME: 15 minutes
SERVES: 4

565 g (1¼ lb) white cabbage
1 eating apple, peeled, cored and roughly chopped
30 g (1 oz) raisins
397 g (14 oz) can chopped tomatoes
½ tsp dried basil
1 clove garlic, chopped
salt and freshly ground black pepper

1. Shred the cabbage and put into a large casserole with the apple.
2. Combine the raisins, chopped tomatoes, basil and garlic. Season lightly and pour over cabbage. Stir.
3. Cover and microwave on 100%/HIGH for 12–15 minutes, or until cabbage is cooked to your liking – stir twice during this time.
4. Allow to stand for 5 minutes before serving.

Haddock Creole

Haddock is an almost perfect food. It is high in protein, calcium and essential vitamins and minerals. It has only traces of fat and is low in calories. This mild fruity curry is delicious served on a bed of brown rice.

PREPARATION TIME: 15 minutes
MICROWAVE COOKING TIME: 13 minutes
SERVES: 4

1 medium onion, chopped
1 large carrot, peeled and diced
1 tbsp mild curry powder
411 g (14½ oz) can apricot halves in natural juice, drained and chopped
397 g (14 oz) can chopped tomatoes
salt and freshly ground black pepper
1 rounded tsp cornflour
½ tsp dried oregano
450 g (1 lb) white haddock fillet
1 tbsp soured cream

TO SERVE
plenty of finely chopped parsley

1. Put the onion and carrot into a medium-sized casserole dish. Cover and microwave on 100%/HIGH for 4 minutes.
2. Stir in the curry powder, the chopped apricots and the can of tomatoes. Season.
3. Mix the cornflour to a smooth paste with 3 tbsp water and stir into the casserole with the oregano.
4. Microwave, uncovered, on 100%/HIGH for 5 minutes, stirring frequently.
5. Cut the fish into cubes and add to the curry sauce. Stir gently.
6. Cover and microwave on 100%/HIGH for 4 minutes.
7. Stir, then stir in soured cream and serve immediately, sprinkled with the finely chopped parsley. Serve with plain brown rice.

PARSLEY PLAICE

Plaice fillets are both delicious and low in calories. They contain protein, calcium, vitamins and minerals. Fish is so quick and easy to cook in the microwave, and this family recipe is a treat for everyone.

PREPARATION TIME: 5 minutes
MICROWAVE COOKING TIME: 6 minutes
SERVES: 4

4 large fillets plaice
30 g (1 oz) butter
1 tsp dried parsley

TO SERVE
sprigs of fresh parsley
lemon wedges

1. Lay the fillets of plaice out flat in a large, shallow dish.
2. Put the butter into a cup and microwave on 40%/SIMMER for 2 minutes, or until melted.
3. Stir parsley into melted butter.
4. Pour over fish. Cover the dish and microwave on 100%/HIGH for 3½–4 minutes.
5. Allow to stand, covered, for 5 minutes, then serve garnished with sprigs of parsley and lemon wedges.

Traditionally plaice was almost always served plainly cooked, as it is cooked here. A little butter is used for its wonderful flavour.

SEAFOOD PANCAKES

Wholemeal flour pancakes have more taste and fibre than those made with plain white flour. Filled with this light yoghurt and mixed fish mixture, they make a delicious special meal, which is quick to prepare if you keep a supply of cooked pancakes in your freezer.

PREPARATION TIME: 20 minutes
MICROWAVE COOKING TIME: 13–17 minutes
SERVES: 4

4 large frozen pancakes, made with wholemeal flour, cooked conventionally, then cooled and layered with baking parchment for the freezer

FOR THE FILLING
4 frozen cod steaks, each weighing 95 g (3¼ oz)
115 g (4 oz) frozen peeled prawns
2 tbsp semi-skimmed milk
salt and freshly ground black pepper
½ tsp dried oregano
140 ml (5 fl oz) natural yoghurt
2 tsp tomato purée
285 ml (½ pt) coating cheese sauce

TO SERVE
fresh parsley sprigs

1. Microwave the frozen pancakes for 5–7 minutes on 30%/DEFROST. Set aside.
2. Defrost the cod steaks by placing them in a ring on a large plate and microwaving on 40%/SIMMER for 5–7 minutes. Turn each steak over after 3 minutes. Set aside for 5 minutes to complete defrosting (see note).
3. If the prawns are frozen, defrost in the microwave (see p. 27).
4. Prepare the filling. Put the defrosted cod steaks into a microwave loaf pan. Add the milk. Season with a little sea salt and some freshly ground black pepper. Sprinkle over the oregano. Cover and microwave on 100%/HIGH for 3–4 minutes, or until fish is no longer opaque. Set aside.
5. Put the prawns and the natural yoghurt into a mixing bowl. Retaining the juices, flake in the cooked, drained fish. Mix well, adding the tomato purée and a little seasoning.
6. Divide the filling evenly between the pancakes, and roll each one up.
7. Arrange over the base of a shallow serving dish. Beat any juices from the fish into the cheese sauce, then microwave the sauce for about 2 minutes on 100%/HIGH to re-heat it. Stir and pour evenly over the pancakes.
8. Cover and microwave on 100%/HIGH for 3–4 minutes, or until heated through.
9. Serve immediately, garnished with the sprigs of fresh parsley.

NOTE: The cod steaks may be cooked from frozen on 100%/HIGH if necessary, but the results are better if they are defrosted first.

Pancakes were always served as a pudding, particularly on Shrove Tuesday, when they are traditionally finished with castor sugar and lemon juice. As they freeze well, making them into delicious savoury meals is quick and easy. The wholemeal flour variety have more food value. They are also easier to cook and handle!

SUMMER SALMON

Nothing could be more traditional in late June and July than fresh whole salmon, stuffed with fresh herbs and garnished with cucumber and strawberries. The microwave deals beautifully with salmon, which must be curled round to fit on to the turntable. It then, obviously, must be served in the curved shape when cooked and skinned, but this method is far more acceptable than cooking the fish in two halves. Hollandaise sauce or mayonnaise will best complement the salmon.

PREPARATION TIME: 10 minutes
MICROWAVE COOKING TIME: 36 minutes
SERVES: 12

1 × 1.8 kg (4 lb) salmon, weighed after a gutting
melted butter for brushing
fresh herbs, e.g. rosemary, sage, thyme, parsley
salt and freshly ground black pepper

TO GARNISH
1 cucumber
fresh strawberries
watercress

1. Brush the salmon all over with a little melted butter.
2. Insert the herbs where the fishmonger has gutted the fish. Season lightly.
3. Mask the head and thin tail areas with tin foil. Cover this

foil with clingfilm so that the foil cannot accidentally touch the oven's sides.

4. Find the fin that protrudes at the top of the fish and, with a sharp knife, make a slit either side of this fin, about 2.5 cm (1″) long so that the steam will be able to escape.
5. Curve the fish round to fit inside turntable. If your oven does not have a turntable, cook the salmon on a large, round plate.
6. Calculate the cooking time, allowing 8–9 minutes per 450 g (1 lb). Therefore, a 4 lb salmon will take 36 minutes approximately.
7. Set the microwave to SIMMER, and cook the salmon for half the total cooking time, i.e. 18 minutes.
8. Remove clingfilm and foil and continue to microwave on SIMMER for remainder of calculated time, i.e. 18 minutes.
9. Allow to stand for 5 minutes, then test salmon by putting a sharp knife into the slit made earlier. The knife should go in easily.
10. Peel away the skin and serve the salmon hot with hollandaise sauce or cold with mayonnaise. Garnish with slices of cucumber, sliced strawberries and watercress.

STUFFED TROUT

English river trout, readily available throughout the year, are a little smaller than sea trout but have a delicious and delicate flavour. Here they are filled with prawns mixed with breadcrumbs and lemon, and covered with cream to finish. Remember to choose a dish that will go under the grill after microwaving.

PREPARATION TIME: 15 minutes
MICROWAVE COOKING TIME: 12 minutes
SERVES: 4

1 small onion, finely chopped
1 tbsp chopped parsley
55 g (2 oz) cottage cheese

55 g (2 oz) frozen prawns, defrosted and chopped
1 tsp lemon juice
1 egg yolk
55 g (2 oz) + 2 tbsp fresh brown breadcrumbs
salt and freshly ground black pepper
4 trout, cleaned and gutted, about 150 g (6 oz) each
55 g (2 oz) polyunsaturated margarine
2 cloves garlic, crushed
142 ml (5 fl oz) carton Shape (reduced-fat) single cream

TO SERVE
lemon wedges
sprigs of parsley

1. Put the chopped onion into a medium-sized mixing bowl. Cover and microwave on 100%/HIGH for 1 minute.
2. Allow to stand for 1 minute, then stir in the parsley, cottage cheese, prawns, lemon juice, egg yolk and 2 oz breadcrumbs. Season with a little salt and pepper and mix well.
3. Divide the mixture between the cavities of each fish.
4. Put the margarine and garlic into a suitable shallow dish and microwave, uncovered, on 100%/HIGH for 1½ minutes, or until melted and hot. Arrange the prepared fish, nose to tail, in the melted margarine. Using a pastry brush, brush the margarine and garlic all over the fish.
5. Cover and microwave on 100%/HIGH for 8 minutes.
6. Pour the cream over the cooked trout and sprinkle with 2 tbsp breadcrumbs. Microwave on 100%/HIGH for 2 minutes, then brown under a pre-heated grill before serving, garnished with the lemon wedges and sprigs of parsley.

COD WITH CIDER AND MUSTARD

Plump cod steaks served with a cider and mustard sauce and garnished with capers comprise a traditional dish that is light and nutritious.

PREPARATION TIME: 10 minutes
MICROWAVE COOKING TIME: 16 minutes
SERVES: 4

1 medium carrot, peeled and cut into matchsticks
1 small onion, chopped
1 celery stick, chopped
1 bayleaf
285 ml (½ pt) dry cider or apple juice
4 cod steaks, 170 g (6 oz) each
pinch of salt and freshly ground black pepper
3 tsp coarse-grain French mustard
4 rounded tsp cornflour

TO SERVE
plenty of finely chopped parsley
a few capers

1. Put the carrot, onion, celery and bayleaf into a medium-sized casserole. Add 2 tbsp of the cider. Cover and microwave on 100%/HIGH for 4 minutes. Stir.
2. Lay the cod steaks on top of the vegetables. Pour over the remaining cider or apple juice. Season. Cover and microwave on 100%/HIGH for about 6–8 minutes, or until cod flakes easily.
3. Lift the steaks on to a warm serving dish and set aside, covered.
4. Stir the mustard into the vegetables and cider. Cream the cornflour to a smooth paste with a little water and stir into the vegetables. Microwave, uncovered, on 100%/HIGH for 3–4 minutes, stirring frequently. The sauce must boil and thicken.
5. Pour the sauce over the cod steaks and serve immediately, sprinkled with the chopped parsley and capers.

NOTE: You may use cider, apple juice, fish stock or vegetable stock for the liquid in this recipe – all are delicious.

PLAICE IN ORANGE SAUCE

Plaice is abundant in the English Channel. It has a wonderful flavour and is suitable for serving at a dinner party. The mild orange sauce and the cream cheese stuffing add luxury to the dish without making it rich and heavy. Serve with creamed potatoes and a mixed salad.

PREPARATION TIME: 15 minutes
MICROWAVE COOKING TIME: 13 minutes
SERVES: 3–4

4 plaice fillets, skinned
55 g (2 oz) half-fat cream cheese
55 g (2 oz) mushrooms, chopped
2 spring onions, chopped
55 g (2 oz) fresh brown breadcrumbs
grated rind of 1 orange and juice of ½ orange
salt and freshly ground black pepper
60 ml (4 tbsp) dry white wine

FOR THE SAUCE
150 ml (¼ pt) fish or vegetable stock, hot
30 g (1 oz) butter
30 g (1 oz) flour
½ tsp dried parsley

TO GARNISH
slices of fresh orange
sprigs of parsley

1. Cut each fillet of plaice in half lengthwise to give 8 small fillets. Lay the fillets out on a board.
2. To prepare the stuffing, put the cream cheese, chopped mushrooms, onions and breadcrumbs into a bowl. Add half of the grated orange rind and season with a little salt and pepper. Add just enough wine to bind the stuffing (about 1 tbsp) and mix well.
3. Divide the stuffing between the plaice fillets, spreading it out evenly. Roll each fillet up and arrange in a suitable shallow dish. Mix the orange juice into the remaining wine and pour over the fish.
4. Cover and microwave on 100%/HIGH for 5 minutes.
5. Lift the stuffed plaice fillets on to a serving dish, using a fish slice. Cover and set aside to keep warm. Retain cooking liquid and mix with stock.
6. Put the butter into a litre (2 pt) jug and microwave on

100%/HIGH for 1 minute. Stir in the flour, then gradually stir in the stock and cooking liquid.

7. Microwave on 100%/HIGH for 4 minutes, stirring frequently with a wire balloon whisk. Stir in remaining orange rind with the dried parsley.
8. Pour the sauce over the fish. Microwave on 70%/ROAST for 2–3 minutes to re-heat. Garnish with slices of orange and sprigs of parsley. Serve immediately with creamed potatoes and a mixed salad.

HALIBUT AU GRATIN

In season all the year round, halibut is a white fish containing a very good supply of fat-soluble vitamins A and D in the liver (halibut liver oil). Presented on spinach and served with a cheese sauce, this recipe provides a well-balanced main meal. Serve with steamed carrots and wholemeal bread. Choose a container that will go under the grill.

PREPARATION TIME: 25 minutes
MICROWAVE COOKING TIME: 27 minutes
SERVES: 4

2 × 227 g (8 oz) blocks frozen chopped spinach
55 g (2 oz) lean streaky bacon, de-rinded
4 halibut steaks, about 740 g (1 lb 10 oz) total weight
2 tbsp semi-skimmed milk
salt and freshly ground black pepper

FOR THE SAUCE
45 g (1½ oz) butter
45 g (1½ oz) flour
285 ml (½ pt) semi-skimmed milk
1 clove garlic, crushed
85 g (3 oz) Cheddar cheese, grated (low-fat if preferred)
30 g (1 oz) fresh brown breadcrumbs

TO GARNISH
fresh coriander

1. Cut open the packets of spinach, so that it will be easy to remove the spinach when it is cooked. Lay the packets side by side on two sheets of absorbent kitchen paper in a shallow dish.
2. Microwave on 100%/HIGH for 11 minutes, turning each packet over once, halfway through. Drain the spinach well by putting it into a sieve and squeezing out excess water with the back of a spoon.
3. Turn the drained spinach into a serving dish, spreading it out evenly. Cover and set aside.
4. Arrange the bacon on two sheets of absorbent kitchen paper on a dinner plate. Cover with a single sheet of kitchen paper. Microwave on 100%/HIGH for 2 minutes, or until bacon is fairly crisp. Allow to stand for 1–2 minutes. (Remember it will continue to crisp during the standing time.)
5. Snip bacon over spinach. Set aside.
6. To cook the halibut, arrange the steaks in a suitable shallow dish and spoon over the 2 tbsp of milk. Season. Cover and microwave on 100%/HIGH for 5–6 minutes, or until fish flakes easily. Set aside, covered.
7. To make the sauce, put the butter into a litre (2 pt) jug. Microwave for 1 minute on 100%/HIGH. Stir in the flour and then blend in any juices from the cooked fish. Add the 285 ml (½ pt) milk with the crushed garlic. Season.
8. Microwave, uncovered, for 3–4 minutes on 100%/HIGH, stirring frequently with a wire balloon whisk. The sauce must rise right up in the jug and thicken.
9. Stir in 55 g (2 oz) of the cheese until it melts.
10. Flake the cooked halibut steaks on to the spinach and bacon, discarding skin and bones.
11. Pour over the sauce to coat the fish. Combine the breadcrumbs and remaining cheese and sprinkle over the sauce.
12. Return to microwave, uncovered, for about 3 minutes on 100%/HIGH to re-heat, then crisp under a grill and serve immediately, garnished with the coriander.

FISH AND VEGETABLE PIE

Traditional fish pie with added vegetables, made with skimmed milk or fish stock to lighten the sauce. An excellent British 'standby', especially convenient if using frozen cod steaks.

PREPARATION TIME: 20 minutes
MICROWAVE COOKING TIME: 27 minutes
SERVES: 4

4 frozen cod steaks, 100 g (3½ oz) each
2 frozen coley steaks, 100 g (3½ oz) each
3 tbsp skimmed milk
salt and freshly ground black pepper
1 large parsnip, peeled and diced
340 g (12 oz) can asparagus spears, drained and chopped
680 g (1½ lb) cooked potatoes

FOR THE SAUCE
30 g (1 oz) vegetable margarine
45 g (1½ oz) plain flour
285 ml (½ pt) skimmed milk
1 tbsp fresh finely chopped parsley
30 g (1 oz) grated low-fat Cheddar-type cheese

TO GARNISH
a little paprika pepper

1. Remove the frozen cod and coley steaks and arrange in a single layer in the base of a suitable dish.
2. Spoon over 3 tbsp skimmed milk. Season.
3. Cover and microwave on 100%/HIGH for about 10–12 minutes, or until fish flakes. Set aside, covered.
4. Put the diced parsnip into a small casserole. Add 2 tbsp water. Cover and microwave on 100%/HIGH for about 5 minutes, or until tender. Stir and set aside, covered.
5. To make the parsley sauce, put the margarine into a litre (2 pt) jug. Microwave uncovered for 45 seconds, or until hot. Stir in flour. Gradually stir in juices from the fish and the 285 ml (½ pt) milk, but before doing so, take 2 tbsp milk out to mash potatoes with.

6. Microwave the sauce uncovered on 100%/HIGH for 3–4 minutes, stirring frequently with a balloon whisk. The sauce must rise right up in the jug and thicken.
7. Beat in the parsley.
8. Flake the fish into a suitable pie dish. Add the drained parsnips and the drained, chopped asparagus. Pour over the sauce to coat evenly.
9. Mash down the potatoes with the reserved 2 tbsp milk (pop them back into the microwave for 1½ minutes on 100%/HIGH to make mashing easier).
10. Spread the potatoes over the ingredients in the pie dish. Fork up, then pop the pie back into the microwave for about 4 minutes on 100%/HIGH to re-heat. Top with grated cheese and brown under a pre-heated grill.
11. Serve immediately, sprinkled with a little paprika.

Parsnips were usually served with fish on Fridays or boiled beef on Saturdays. They have a slightly sweet flavour, which goes well with the fish and asparagus. The light parsley sauce complements the pie well.

PLAICE WITH ORANGE

Fillets of plaice stuffed with ground almonds, wholemeal breadcrumbs, orange rind and egg, poached in white wine with mixed herbs and served with fresh orange segments and watercress. Excellent served with cooked broccoli and brown rice to which peas and sweetcorn have been added.

PREPARATION TIME: 10–15 minutes
MICROWAVE COOKING TIME: 5 minutes
SERVES: 4

55 g (2 oz) wholemeal breadcrumbs
55 g (2 oz) ground almonds
grated rind of ½ orange
1 egg, beaten, size 4

salt and freshly ground black pepper
8 × 85 g (3 oz) plaice fillets, skinned
1 tbsp orange juice
2 tbsp white wine
1 tsp dried mixed herbs

TO GARNISH
1 orange, segmented
sprigs of fresh watercress
55 g (2 oz) chopped walnuts

1. Prepare filling. Put the breadcrumbs, ground almonds, orange rind and egg into a medium-sized bowl. Mix well to combine. Season lightly.
2. Divide filling between plaice fillets, spreading it fairly thickly over each fish. Roll up, head to tail.
3. Arrange rolled fish close together in a suitable dish.
4. Combine orange juice, white wine and herbs and pour over fish. Cover.
5. Microwave on 100%/HIGH for 5 minutes.
6. Allow to stand for 3 minutes, then, using a draining spoon, lift fish on to serving dish. Garnish with segments of fresh orange and sprigs of watercress and sprinkle over chopped walnuts.

MICROWAVE BAKING

Pizza with pickle
Wholemeal rolls
White milk loaf
Chocolate cherry buns
Victoria sandwich
Apple and blackcurrant flan
Ginger biscuits
Chocolate muesli cake
Wholefood fruit cake
Vegetable cobbler
Spicy almond cake
Cheese scones
Carrot cake with orange frosting
Walnut and apricot bakes
Wine and marmalade cake
Almond biscuits
Banana tea ring
Cinnamon savarin
Meringues with peppermint cream
Pineapple upside-down pudding
Chocolate gâteau
Ground almond shortbread
Rich fruit cake

Microwave bakes are extremely successful, but people often experience some difficulty with this aspect of microwave cookery, probably due to the fact that the cooked item looks somewhat different to its conventionally cooked counterpart.

For this reason and because, once mastered, this quick method of producing bread, biscuits and cakes is fairly foolproof, I have written the recipe instructions in careful detail, explaining how to mix correctly, how long to cook each item and how long to allow for the standing time. The recipes, if followed to the letter, will prove successful. Please note, however, that even microwave ovens of the same wattage differ considerably from manufacturer to manufacturer, and the results of one microwave may be inconsistent with those of another. Therefore, remember to use the timings given as a guide, as your particular oven may cook a little quicker or slower than mine.

The recipes were tested on a Philips 700 W oven with variable power. For ovens of a different power, see p. 16 to calculate correct cooking times.

Baking has, of course, been a British tradition for centuries – the microwave is here to bring it bang up to date. It is fun to discover just how many old recipes may be baked in the microwave in roughly one-third to one-quarter of the time it would take to cook them conventionally. I hope you enjoy trying the recipes as much as I did formulating them.

PIZZA WITH PICKLE

Pizza is a traditional Italian meal, which has recently become very popular in this country, as it provides a nutritious, satisfying meal. It freezes well and may be heated in the microwave, straight from frozen. Serve with a mixed salad.

PREPARATION TIME: 40 minutes plus rising time
MICROWAVE COOKING TIME: 19–22 minutes
SERVES: 6

FOR THE BASE
283 g (10 oz) packet brown bread mix

FOR THE TOPPING
1 medium onion, chopped
397g (14 oz) can chopped tomatoes
½ tsp oregano
4 tbsp piccalilli, or sweet pickle if preferred
salt and freshly ground black pepper
170 g (6 oz) Gouda cheese, grated
50 g (1¾ oz) can anchovies in oil, drained

1. Make up and knead the dough exactly as directed on the packet.
2. Roll out the dough and shape to fit a 25 cm (10″) flat plate. Lightly grease the plate and put the dough on to it. Cover with a damp tea-towel and set aside to rise in a warm place for about 1 hour, or until double in height.
3. Meanwhile, prepare the topping. Put the onion into a 1.7 l (3 pt) mixing bowl. Cover and microwave on 100%/HIGH for 2 minutes. Stir in the chopped tomatoes, oregano and pickle. Season. Microwave on 100%/HIGH, uncovered, for 12–14 minutes, or until reduced to a thick pulp. Stir frequently during this time.
4. Microwave the risen dough for 3 minutes on 100%/HIGH. Spread the reduced topping mixture all over the pizza evenly, then top with the grated cheese. Arrange the drained anchovies in a pattern over the pizza.
5. Microwave on 100%/HIGH for 2–3 minutes, or until cheese melts. Serve immediately.

WHOLEMEAL ROLLS

Bread was baked and eaten in this country as long ago as the Stone and Iron Ages. Today bread is a very important part of our diet, as it supplies more than a quarter of the total energy, protein, carbohydrate and iron eaten in the average household. Wholemeal bread provides also a good source of vitamin B and has more fibre than white bread.

PREPARATION TIME: 35 minutes plus rising time
MICROWAVE COOKING TIME: 6 minutes
MAKES: 12 rolls

450 g (1 lb) 100% wholemeal flour
225 g (8 oz) strong plain white flour
1 tsp salt
30 g (1 oz) margarine
1 tsp sugar
2 level tsp dried baking yeast
beaten egg, to glaze

TO SERVE
buckwheat, for sprinkling

1. Mix the flours and salt, and sieve into a large bowl. Rub in the margarine.
2. Put 115 ml (4 fl oz) of lukewarm water into a jug. Stir in the sugar and yeast. Set aside in a warm place for 15 minutes, or until frothy.
3. Make a 'well' in centre of flour and pour in yeast mixture with a further 310 ml (11 fl oz) of lukewarm water.
4. Mix to an elastic dough. Knead on a floured table for 10 minutes.
5. Put dough in a lightly oiled large bowl. Cover with a clean, damp tea-towel and set aside in a warm place until double in size (about 1 hour).
6. Pull the spongy, risen dough on to a floured surface. Knead well for 5 minutes. Divide dough into 12 even-sized portions and knead into balls.
7. Place the balls of dough, arranged in a ring fashion, on to 2 lightly greased dinner plates. Cover once more with a damp tea-towel and leave in a warm place until double in size (about 20 minutes).
8. Brush the proved rolls with beaten egg and sprinkle with buckwheat, pressing lightly to make it stick.
9. Cook the rolls, 6 at a time, on 100%/HIGH for 2½–3 minutes. When pressed lightly with the finger, the rolls should spring back.
10. Leave to cool on a wire rack.

WHITE MILK LOAF

Butter, milk and eggs were added to basic bread dough very early on by dedicated cooks trying to improve what was probably the most important item in their diet. Milk loaf keeps well, and although when cooked in the microwave it will not have a crisp crust, it may be sprinkled with the poppy seeds before baking to improve the appearance. This bread is delicious toasted.

PREPARATION TIME: 25 minutes plus rising time
MICROWAVE COOKING TIME: 6 minutes
MAKES: 1 loaf

450 g (1 lb) strong plain white flour
1 level tsp salt
285 ml (½ pt) milk
1 level tsp sugar
2 level tsp dried yeast
a little beaten egg to glaze

TO SERVE
poppy seeds for sprinkling (optional)

1. Sieve flour and salt into a bowl. Make a well in the centre.
2. Microwave the milk in a ½ l (1 pt) jug for about 1½ mins on 100%/HIGH, or until warm. Dissolve the sugar in the warm milk, then stir in the yeast. Set aside for 15 minutes, or until mixture froths.
3. Add the yeast mixture to the flour, mixing thoroughly until a dough is formed.
4. Turn on to a lightly floured board and knead for 10 minutes until you have a smooth elastic dough.
5. Wash up the mixing bowl and lightly oil it. Put the dough into the bowl. Cover with a damp tea-towel and set aside in a warm place until the dough doubles in size (about 1 hour).
6. Turn the dough out on to the floured surface and knead again to knock out the air bubbles – about 5 minutes.
7. Lightly oil a 1.4 l (2½ pt) microwave loaf dish.

8. Shape the bread and place the dough in the loaf tin. Cover again with the damp tea-towel and set aside in a warm place until the dough rises above the top of the dish (15–20 minutes).
9. Brush the top of the loaf with beaten egg and sprinkle with poppy seeds.
10. Microwave, uncovered, on 100%/HIGH for about 6 minutes, or until bread is well risen and just 'set'. When pressed lightly with a finger, the bread should spring back.
11. Turn out on to a cooling rack and allow to cool completely.

NOTE: Best stored in tupperware container in refrigerator. Will keep 2–3 days.

CHOCOLATE CHERRY BUNS

Tea first became popular in this country during the reign of Charles II, and the custom of serving 'afternoon tea', with bread and butter and cake, developed gradually over the years. Fairy cakes are a traditional tea-time treat; try this chocolate version made spicy with a little cinnamon. The chopped glacé cherries will add appeal for children.

PREPARATION TIME: 5 minutes
MICROWAVE COOKING TIME: 6 minutes
MAKES: 16 buns

6 or 12 paper fairy-cake cases (see step 5)

115 g (4 oz) castor sugar
115 g (4 oz) soft margarine
85 g (3 oz) self-raising flour
30 g (1 oz) cocoa
½ tsp cinnamon, optional
2 large eggs
2 tbsp milk
55 g (2 oz) glacé cherries, washed and chopped

1. Cream the sugar and margarine until light and fluffy.
2. Sieve together the flour, cocoa and cinnamon.
3. Beat together the eggs and milk, then, using a wooden spoon, gradually beat the eggs and milk into the margarine and sugar, adding a spoonful of the sifted flour and cocoa now and again to prevent the mixture from curdling.
4. Fold in remaining flour and cocoa and then the prepared cherries.
5. Arrange 1 paper fairy-cake case in each of the 6 holes in a microwave egg-poacher, or arrange 6 double paper cases in a ring on a dinner plate.
6. Put 1 dessertspoonful of the mixture into each case. Level surface. Microwave, uncovered, on 100%/HIGH for 2¼ minutes. Allow cakes to stand for 2 minutes, then transfer them to a wire cooling tray.
7. Continue with this method until all the mixture has been used up. The last 4 buns should be microwaved for about 1½ minutes only.

NOTE: Take great care not to overcook these cakes or they will dry out and be very hard! They may be topped with a little melted chocolate before serving.

VICTORIA SANDWICH

As the name suggests, Victoria sandwich was first prepared for Queen Victoria in the late nineteenth century. She obviously enjoyed eating the cake very much, as she often requested that it be baked for the tea parties she gave. It was usually filled with raspberry jam, but try this almond version made with low-fat spread and filled with apricot jam.

PREPARATION TIME: 15 minutes
MICROWAVE COOKING TIME: 10 minutes
MAKES: 6–8 slices

castor sugar for preparing the dish

170 g (6 oz) low-fat spread, at room temperature
170 g (6 oz) castor sugar
170 g (6 oz) self-raising flour, sieved
a few drops almond essence (optional)
½ tsp baking powder
3 large eggs, size 2
2 tbsp semi-skimmed milk

FOR THE FILLING
2–3 tablespoons reduced-sugar apricot jam

TO SERVE
castor sugar

1. Lightly oil a deep 19 cm (7½″) soufflé dish. Line the base with a circle of greaseproof paper and dust the sides with a little castor sugar.
2. Put all the ingredients for the cake into a mixing bowl and mix with a wooden spoon to combine, then beat for about 1 minute.
3. Transfer the mixture to the prepared soufflé dish. Level surface.
4. Microwave, uncovered, on 70%/ROAST for 7 minutes, then continue to microwave on 100%/HIGH for 2–3 minutes, or until cake has risen right to the top of the container and is just set. A wooden cocktail stick inserted into the centre of the cake should come out clean. Allow to stand in container for 10–15 minutes, then turn out on to a cooling rack, which is covered with 2 sheets of absorbent kitchen paper sprinkled with a little castor sugar (this will prevent cake from sticking). Allow to cool completely.
5. Cut cake through the middle, fill with jam, then sandwich together and serve sprinkled with a little castor sugar.

NOTE: Owing to the use of low-fat spread, this cake will only keep fresh and moist in an airtight tin for about 2 days. It is, however, considerably lower in fat than the conventional version and just as delicious.

Apple and Blackcurrant Flan

Blackcurrants have long been recognized for their high vitamin C content. They, like nearly all fruits and vegetables, are also high in fibre. This attractive flan is delicious served cold with ice-cream or natural yoghurt.

PREPARATION TIME: 25 minutes
MICROWAVE COOKING TIME: 17 minutes
SERVES: 6

115 g (4 oz) polyunsaturated margarine, cold from fridge
1 egg yolk
115 g (4 oz) plain flour, sieved
115 g (4 oz) plain wholemeal flour, sieved with bran residue added

FOR THE FILLING
450 g (1 lb) fresh or frozen blackcurrants
85 g (3 oz) soft brown sugar
2 tsp arrowroot
3 green-skinned eating apples
3 red-skinned eating apples
lemon juice for brushing sliced apples
3 tbsp raspberry jam

1. To make the pastry, put the margarine into a mixing bowl and microwave on 100%/HIGH for 10–12 *seconds*. Whip up with a fork.
2. Add 3 tbsp cold water, the egg yolk and one third of the flour. Mix with a fork until all ingredients are combined. Add remaining flour and continue to mix until a pliable dough is formed, eventually using your hands.
3. Knead on a lightly floured board, then roll out and use to line a 25 cm (10″) fluted plastic or pottery pie dish. Refrigerate for 30 minutes.
4. Meanwhile prepare the filling. Put the blackcurrants and sugar into a large casserole. Cover and microwave on 100%/HIGH for 6–7 minutes, a little longer if fruit is frozen. Stir and re-cover halfway through cooking time. Blend arrow-

root with a little water and add to blackcurrants. Cover and microwave on 100%/HIGH for 1–2 minutes. Stir.

5. Prick the base and sides of the flan all over with a fork. Put 2 sheets absorbent kitchen paper in the base of the flan and microwave on 100%/HIGH for 4 minutes, then remove paper and continue to microwave on 100%/HIGH for 3 minutes, or until pastry is dry.
6. Turn cooled blackcurrants into base of flan. (Transfer the flan to a serving dish first if you are using a plastic flan ring with a removable base.)
7. Core each apple, then cut into thin, even slices.
8. Paint the apple slices on both sides with lemon juice. I find this easy to do if I put the lemon juice in a cereal bowl (about 2–3 tbsp) and then briefly soak the apple slices, a few at a time, in the bowl.
9. Arrange the prepared slices in an attractive wheel-like pattern around the flan, starting on the outside edge and working towards the centre. Use 1 red slice, then 1 green in sequence, slightly overlapping. The slices should eventually completely cover the blackcurrant filling.
10. Lastly prepare the glaze. Put the jam into a mug and microwave on 100%/HIGH for about 1 minute. Stir, then pass through a clean tea-strainer into a small bowl. Carefully brush slices all over with the prepared glaze. Serve cold.

GINGER BISCUITS

Spicy, crunchy biscuits made from wholemeal flour and low-fat spread, which reduces the rather high fat content of traditional biscuits, are very moreish! These biscuits do spread a little on baking, so allow for this. They also harden while standing, so take care not to overcook them initially.

PREPARATION TIME: 15 minutes
MICROWAVE COOKING TIME: about 8 minutes
MAKES: 24 biscuits

225 g (8 oz) self-raising wholemeal flour
2 tsp ginger
115 g (4 oz) low-fat spread
55 g (2 oz) soft light brown sugar
1 level tbsp golden syrup
1 egg, beaten

1. Sieve flour and ginger into a large mixing bowl, then add what is left in the sieve.
2. Rub in the low-fat spread until mixture resembles fine breadcrumbs.
3. Stir in brown sugar. Add the golden syrup and beaten egg and combine mixture to form a dough.
4. Divide mixture into 24 balls. Place 6 at a time in a circle on a lightly greased large flat plate. Press each biscuit down firmly with the back of a fork.
5. Microwave on 100%/HIGH for 1¾–2¼ minutes, or until the biscuits are just 'set'. The biscuits firm and crisp on standing, so do not overcook.
6. Remove from microwave and allow biscuits to stand for 10 minutes before transferring to a wire cooling tray.
7. Repeat with remaining mixture.

NOTE: These biscuits will store for a few days in an airtight container.

CHOCOLATE MUESLI CAKE

Oats were among the earliest crops to be grown by man, and oatmeal has long been used as a filler, often served in the evening with warm milk and sugar or honey.

Muesli as we know it today has been in and out of fashion for many years. It is a particularly healthy way to start the day when served with semi-skimmed or skimmed milk. In this recipe, Jordans' crunchy cereal is used to make a delicious but calorie-laden tea-time treat!

PREPARATION TIME: 15 minutes
MICROWAVE COOKING TIME: 9–10 minutes
MAKES: 8–10 slices

200 g (7 oz) milk chocolate
115 g (4 oz) vegetable margarine
2 level tsp cocoa powder
115 g (4 oz) broken digestive biscuits
115 g (4 oz) Jordans' Original Crunchy cereal
55 g (2 oz) chopped walnuts
55 g (2 oz) glacé cherries, washed and chopped
30 g (1 oz) raisins

1. Break the chocolate into pieces and put it into a 1.7 l (3 pt) mixing bowl.
2. Microwave, uncovered, on 40%/SIMMER, *stirring frequently*, for 5–6 minutes, or until almost fully melted. Add the margarine and microwave on 40%/SIMMER, *stirring frequently*, for about 4 minutes, or until melted.
3. Stir all remaining ingredients into chocolate and margarine, mixing well until thoroughly combined.
4. Turn into a lightly greased re-usable 1.7 l (3 pt) loaf pan. Level the surface, then refrigerate overnight.
5. To serve, loosen the edge with a round-bladed knife, then turn on to a serving dish.
6. Serve immediately, cut into small cubes, as the cake is very rich.

NOTE: This cake is also very successful made with carob chips instead of chocolate; follow instructions exactly as given.

WHOLEFOOD FRUIT CAKE

A high-fibre cake made from wholemeal flour and sunflower margarine with coconut, walnuts, dried apricots and dates. Little sugar is needed to sweeten this delicious rich fruit cake, which is cooked to moist perfection using the SIMMER control on your microwave. Fruit cake has been popular in England since the seventeenth century.

PREPARATION TIME: 15 minutes
MICROWAVE COOKING TIME: 20–23 minutes
MAKES: 12 slices

225 g (8 oz) self-raising wholemeal flour
170 g (6 oz) polyunsaturated margarine, cold from fridge
55 g (2 oz) soft dark brown sugar
55 g (2 oz) desiccated coconut
55 g (2 oz) dried apricots, chopped
55 g (2 oz) walnuts, chopped
55 g (2 oz) stoned dates, chopped
3 eggs, size 3
3 tbsp semi-skimmed milk

TO SERVE
2 tbsp apricot jam
6 walnut halves

1. Lightly grease a 23 cm (9″) microwave ring mould.
2. Sieve the flour into a large mixing bowl. Rub in the margarine, then add the sugar, coconut, dried apricots, walnuts and dates. Mix lightly.
3. Beat together the eggs and milk and add to the dry ingredients. Mix well to combine.
4. Turn into prepared ring mould. Level surface.
5. Microwave, uncovered, on 40%/SIMMER for 20–23 minutes. Give the container a quarter-turn 3 or 4 times during cooking.
6. Remove from the microwave and allow to stand for 10 minutes.
7. Turn on to 2 sheets of absorbent paper, which have been arranged on a wire cooling rack and sprinkled with a little castor sugar. Leave to cool.
8. When quite cold, arrange on a serving dish.
9. Put the apricot jam into a small dish and microwave on 100%/HIGH for 1 minute. Stir, then pass through a sieve.
10. Using a pastry brush, brush the sieved apricot jam all over the cake to act as a glaze. Decorate with the walnut halves and serve immediately, cut into slices and arranged on a serving dish.

NOTE: This cake keeps well in an airtight tin.

VEGETABLE COBBLER

A filling vegetable stew with a baked scone topping. This popular and traditional lunch or supper dish provides protein both in the sweetcorn and in the cheese scone topping. A particularly healthy microwave bake, suitable for vegetarians.

PREPARATION TIME: 20 minutes
MICROWAVE COOKING TIME: 28 minutes
SERVES: 4

1 medium onion, chopped
340 g (12 oz) courgettes, sliced
2 carrots, peeled and diced
2 small turnips, peeled and diced
1 red pepper, de-seeded and chopped
285 ml (½ pt) well-flavoured vegetable stock, warm
1 tsp dried parsley
450 g (1 lb) tomatoes, peeled and chopped
1 bayleaf
55 g (2 oz) frozen sweetcorn kernels
2 tbsp cornflour
salt and freshly ground black pepper

FOR THE TOPPING
45 g (1½ oz) vegetable margarine, cold from fridge
170 g (6 oz) self-raising wholemeal flour
55 g (2 oz) grated vegetarian Cheddar
milk for mixing

TO SERVE
a little extra grated cheese

1. Put the onion into a large casserole. Cover and microwave on 100%/HIGH for 2 minutes.
2. Add the courgettes, carrots, turnips and red pepper. Stir.
3. Pour over the stock and add the parsley with the chopped tomatoes. Lay the bayleaf on the top.
4. Cover and microwave on 100%/HIGH for 16 minutes, stirring and re-covering after 6 minutes. Stir in sweetcorn. Re-cover.
5. Allow to stand for 2 minutes.
6. Mix the cornflour to a smooth paste with a little water and stir into the casserole.

7. Microwave, uncovered, for 4 minutes, stirring frequently. Season to taste. Remove bayleaf and discard.
8. Prepare the cobbler topping. In a mixing bowl, rub the margarine into the flour. Fork in the cheese and mix to a firm dough with a little milk.
9. Knead lightly, then roll out to a thickness of about 1 cm (½″).
10. Cut into 8 scones and arrange them evenly over the vegetables.
11. Microwave, uncovered, for 5–6 minutes, or until scones are cooked.
12. Serve immediately, sprinkled with a little extra cheese.

NOTE: As long as a grill-proof casserole dish is chosen for this recipe, the dish may be popped under a pre-heated grill for a few minutes just before serving, to crisp and brown the scones.

SPICY ALMOND CAKE

High-fibre almonds with their delicious flavour help to make a moist cake. Brown sugar and wholemeal flour give the cake a good colour and wholemeal flour is more healthy than its white counterpart. The cake keeps well in an airtight tin.

PREPARATION TIME: 10 minutes
MICROWAVE COOKING TIME: 18–20 minutes
MAKES: 10 slices

115 g (4 oz) polyunsaturated margarine
115 (4 oz) dark soft brown sugar
2 tbsp runny honey
3 eggs, size 3
3 tbsp semi-skimmed milk
225 g (8 oz) self-raising wholemeal flour
½ tsp ground nutmeg
½ tsp ground cinnamon
½ tsp ground ginger
} sieved together
115 g (4 oz) blanched almonds, chopped
55 g (2 oz) glacé cherries, washed and chopped

1. Lightly grease a 23 cm (9″) microwave ring mould.
2. Beat the margarine, sugar and honey until light and fluffy. Beat in the eggs one at a time, adding 1 tbsp flour with each egg to prevent mixture curdling. Beat in milk.
3. Fold in flour and spices with the almonds and cherries. Mix well, then turn into prepared ring mould. Level surface. Microwave, uncovered, on 40%/SIMMER for 18–20 minutes, turning a quarter-turn 3–4 times during baking.
4. Remove from microwave and allow to stand in container for 10 minutes.
5. Turn out on to 2 sheets of absorbent kitchen paper, which have been arranged on a wire cooling rack and sprinkled with a little castor sugar. Allow to become quite cold before serving.

NOTE: When cool, the cake can be iced with a white glacé icing.

CHEESE SCONES

Cheese scones made from wholemeal flour and Cheddar cheese are high in fibre and have a wonderful taste and flavour. They may be browned under a pre-heated grill for a few minutes after microwaving, if required.

PREPARATION TIME: 15 minutes
MICROWAVE COOKING TIME: 7–8 minutes
MAKES: 7 large scones

225 g (8 oz) self-raising wholemeal flour
½ tsp baking powder
55 g (2 oz) polyunsaturated margarine, cold from fridge
55 g (2 oz) mature Cheddar cheese, grated
½ tsp dried parsley
1 tsp coarse-grain mustard
semi-skimmed milk for mixing

1. Put the flour and baking powder into a medium-sized mixing bowl. Rub in the margarine until the mixture resembles

fine breadcrumbs. Fork in the cheese and parsley. Add the mustard and enough milk to make an elastic dough.

2. Knead lightly and roll out to a thickness of about 2.5 cm (1″). Cut into 9 scones, using a floured cutter.
3. Arrange the scones in a ring fashion, leaving a gap in the centre, on a large flat plate, grill-proof if necessary (see note).
4. Microwave, uncovered, for 7–8 minutes on 70%/ROAST.
5. Allow to stand for 2 minutes, then brown under a pre-heated grill, if required, before serving. Best served warm.

NOTE: Make sure you use a grill-proof plate if the scones are to be 'browned' under the grill, and brush over with a little milk before browning. If you prefer not to heat the grill, brush the scones with a teaspoon of beef extract, such as Bovril, diluted with a tiny amount of water, before microwaving.

CARROT CAKE WITH ORANGE FROSTING

Grated carrot, as well as providing vitamin A, helps to keep this cake moist. A delicious tea-time treat made from wholemeal flour and dark brown sugar.

PREPARATION TIME: 15 minutes
MICROWAVE COOKING TIME: 10 minutes
MAKES: 6–8 slices

115 g (4 oz) polyunsaturated margarine
85 g (3 oz) soft dark brown sugar
2 eggs, size 4, beaten
55 g (2 oz) desiccated coconut
170 g (6 oz) carrots, finely grated
115 g (4 oz) self-raising wholemeal flour } sieved
1 tsp mixed spice } together

FOR THE FROSTING
115 g (4 oz) low-fat soft cheese (cold from the refrigerator)
55 g (2 oz) soft light brown sugar
grated rind of 1 orange

TO DECORATE
1 orange

1. Lightly oil a re-usable 1.4 l (2½ pt) microwave loaf pan and line the bottom with greaseproof paper. Do not grease paper.
2. Using a wooden spoon, beat together the margarine and brown sugar until light and fluffy. Beat in the eggs gradually. Fold in the coconut and grated carrot. Lastly, using a metal tablespoon, fold in the wholemeal flour with the mixed spice.
3. Transfer mixture to prepared loaf pan. Level surface. Microwave, uncovered, on 70%/ROAST for 10 minutes, turning the dish a quarter-turn 3 times during cooking.
4. Allow to stand in container for 20 minutes, then turn out and allow to cool.
5. When cold, prepare the frosting. Beat together the soft cheese, sugar and orange rind with a wooden spoon. Spread all over the cake.
6. Peel and segment orange, discarding all pith and peel. Arrange orange segments attractively down centre of cake. Serve immediately.

WALNUT AND APRICOT BAKES

From the Middle Ages, biscuits were enjoyed by rich and poor alike, although biscuits with dried apricots and walnuts would have been well out of the reach of poor people. These biscuits are finished with a coating of chocolate, which is popular with children and adults alike.

PREPARATION TIME: 20 minutes
MICROWAVE COOKING TIME: 7 minutes
MAKES: 24 biscuits

115 g (4 oz) vegetable margarine
115 g (4 oz) soft brown sugar
½ a beaten egg
225 g (8 oz) plain flour, sieved
30 g (1 oz) chopped walnuts
55 g (2 oz) chopped dried apricots
115 g (4 oz) dark cooking chocolate

1. Cream the margarine and sugar until light and fluffy.
2. Beat in the egg, then fold in the flour, walnuts and dried apricots. Mix well until a fairly stiff dough is formed.
3. Roll the dough out to a thickness of about 3 mm (⅛″) and cut into 5 cm (2″) rounds.
4. Arrange 8 at a time in a ring fashion on a lightly greased flat dinner plate.
5. Microwave on 100%/HIGH for 2–2½ minutes, or until the biscuits are just firm to the touch.
6. Allow to stand for 5 minutes, then transfer to a wire cooling rack.
7. Repeat until all the mixture has been used up.
8. When the biscuits are cold, break the chocolate into pieces and place in a small bowl. Microwave, uncovered, on 40%/SIMMER, stirring frequently, for 5–7 minutes, or until chocolate has melted.
9. Spread the melted chocolate on to the back of each biscuit, and when it is on the point of setting, mark an attractive pattern with a fork. (I usually coat 3 or 4 biscuits, then go back to the first one and make the pattern.)

NOTE: The biscuits crisp on cooling, so be careful not to overcook them.

WINE AND MARMALADE CAKE

A superbly moist cake made from sunflower oil and wholemeal flour with wine and marmalade. Delicious with or without its low-fat frosting.

PREPARATION TIME: 15 minutes
MICROWAVE COOKING TIME: 13–16 minutes
MAKES: 8–10 slices

140 ml (¼ pt) sunflower oil
140 g (5 oz) soft dark brown sugar
3 large eggs
2 tbsp medium-cut breakfast marmalade
170 g (6 oz) plain wholemeal flour
1 tsp bicarbonate of soda
1 tsp baking powder
1 tsp mixed spice
85 ml (3 fl oz) medium white wine
} **sieved together**

FOR THE FROSTING
85 g (3 oz) Quark low-fat soft cheese
grated rind of 1 orange
115 g (4 oz) sieved icing sugar

TO DECORATE
segments of fresh orange with no pith, peel or skin.

1. Beat together the oil, sugar and eggs, using an electric mixer, for about 2 minutes, or until smooth and glossy.
2. Beat in the marmalade. Add remaining ingredients, folding them in with a tablespoon.
3. Transfer to a greased 23 cm (9″) microwave ring mould.
4. Microwave, uncovered, on 50%/MEDIUM for 9 minutes, then continue to microwave on 100%/HIGH for 4–7 minutes. The cake should be well risen and just firm to the touch.
5. Allow to stand in container for 10 minutes, then lay 2 sheets of absorbent kitchen paper on a metal cooling rack and sprinkle them with a little castor sugar. Turn the cake out on to this. Allow to become quite cold.
6. To make the frosting, put the Quark into a medium-sized mixing bowl and microwave on 100%/HIGH for 8–10 seconds. Beat in the orange rind with the sieved icing sugar.
7. To serve, arrange cake on serving dish and pipe swirls of frosting on top and around base of cake. Decorate with segments of fresh orange.

ALMOND BISCUITS

Make a batch of these biscuits and then a batch of the chocolate cookies on page 120 to present an attractive plate of homemade biscuits at coffee- or tea-time.

PREPARATION TIME: 10 minutes
MICROWAVE COOKING TIME: 4 minutes
MAKES: 12 biscuits

85 g (3 oz) polyunsaturated margarine
55 g (2 oz) soft light brown sugar
1 egg, size 3, beaten
a few drops almond essence
115 g (4 oz) self-raising flour, sieved
55 g (2 oz) almond nibs

1. Beat together the margarine and sugar until light and fluffy. Gradually beat in the egg and almond essence.
2. Work in the sieved flour and the almond nibs.
3. Take teaspoonfuls of the mixture and roll into balls, each about the size of a small walnut.
4. Position 6 at a time on a lightly greased dinner plate, in a ring fashion.
5. Flatten each one slightly with the back of a fork.
6. Microwave each plateful separately, uncovered, on 100%/HIGH for about 2 minutes.
7. Allow to stand for 5 minutes, then transfer to wire cooling rack.

NOTE: These biscuits crisp on cooling, so be careful not to overcook them.

BANANA TEA RING

Traditionally tea breads are cooked in loaf tins, but as it is sometimes difficult to ensure that the centre of the loaf is cooked, I suggest that you make this moist bread in a ring mould. The orange glacé icing gives an attractive optional finish.

PREPARATION TIME: 15 minutes
MICROWAVE COOKING TIME: 11 minutes
MAKES: 6–8 slices

55 ml (2 fl oz) vegetable oil
140 g (5 oz) soft dark brown sugar
2 eggs, size 2, lightly beaten
grated rind of 1 large orange
2 ripe bananas, peeled and mashed
200 g (7 oz) self-raising wholemeal flour } sieved
2 tsp mixed spice } together with

FOR THE ICING
115 g (4 oz) sifted icing sugar
about 1 tbsp hot water
grated rind of ½ orange
15 g (½ oz) butter

1. Beat the oil, brown sugar, eggs, orange rind and mashed bananas until smooth.
2. Stir in the flour and mixed spice, adding bran residue.
3. Turn into a lightly oiled 18 cm (7″) microwave re-usable ring mould.
4. Microwave, uncovered, on 40%/SIMMER for 8 minutes, giving the dish half a turn twice during this time.
5. Then microwave on 100%/HIGH for 2–3 minutes, or until the tea bread is just set.
6. Leave to stand for 5–10 minutes, then turn out on to a wire cooling rack, which has been covered with 2 sheets of absorbent kitchen roll and sprinkled with a little castor sugar. Allow to become quite cold.
7. To make the icing, blend the icing sugar with sufficient hot

water to make a smooth icing. Beat in the orange grated rind and butter.

8. Arrange the tea bread on a serving dish and pour the icing evenly over. Cut into slices and serve as soon as the icing has set.

CINNAMON SAVARIN

Spicy savarin steeped in a rum sugar syrup and filled with fresh orange and kiwi fruit. A deliciously naughty sweet. Serve with natural yoghurt or reduced-fat single cream instead of the traditional whipped double cream.

PREPARATION TIME: 20 minutes plus rising time
MICROWAVE COOKING TIME: 18 minutes
SERVES: 6–8

FOR THE SAVARIN
6 tbsp milk
1 tsp dried yeast
1 tsp castor sugar
55 g (2 oz) butter
115 g (4 oz) plain flour
1 tsp cinnamon
2 eggs, size 3, beaten

FOR THE SYRUP
170 g (6 oz) castor sugar
grated rind of ½ orange
3 tbsp rum

TO GLAZE
4 tbsp apricot jam

TO FILL SAVARIN
3 large oranges
3 kiwi fruit

1. Microwave the milk in a small mixing bowl for 30 seconds on 100%/HIGH. Stir in yeast and sugar and set aside for about 15 minutes until frothy.
2. Put the butter into a cereal bowl and microwave on 40%/SIMMER for 2–2½ minutes until melted. Set aside.

3. Sieve flour and cinnamon into large mixing bowl. Make well in centre and pour in frothy yeast mixture.
4. Beat together eggs and add to mixing bowl with the melted butter. Beat well until a smooth batter results. This will take about 10 minutes using a wooden spoon.
5. Pour into a lightly oiled 18 cm (7″) re-usable ring mould.
6. Cover and leave to prove until dough rises to within ¼″ of the top of the mould. (This will take about an hour, depending on the temperature of the room.)
7. Microwave, uncovered, on 100%/HIGH for 3 minutes, or until savarin is set. Allow to stand for 4 minutes, then turn out on to serving dish.
8. Put sugar, 285 ml (½ pt) water and orange rind into a litre (2 pt) jug and microwave on 100%/HIGH for about 9 minutes, stirring after 3 minutes to ensure sugar has dissolved.
9. Stir in rum.
10. Using a tablespoon, spoon the syrup slowly and evenly on to the savarin, which will rapidly soak it up.
11. Put the apricot jam into ½ l (1 pt) jug. Add 2 tbsp water. Microwave on 70%/ROAST for 2–3 minutes. Stir well, then pass through a sieve.
12. Using a pastry brush, brush the warm apricot glaze all over the savarin.
13. Peel and slice kiwi fruit and peel and segment orange, discarding all pith and peel. Fill the centre of the savarin with the fruit, piling it up attractively, and serve immediately with yoghurt or reduced-fat single cream.

NOTE: Any sugar syrup that is left over may be stored in the fridge when quite cold and used as the base for a fruit salad.

MERINGUES WITH PEPPERMINT CREAM

Microwave meringues are different in texture to those that have been cooked conventionally. As they dry out completely in the microwave, watch your timing, as they can overcook – brown spots will appear in the centre. Once cooled, these meringues are delicious filled with peppermint butter cream.

PREPARATION TIME: 15 minutes
MICROWAVE COOKING TIME: about 5 minutes
MAKES: 10 meringues

1 egg white, size 2
11–12 tbsp sieved icing sugar

FOR THE PEPPERMINT BUTTER CREAM
115 g (4 oz) polyunsaturated margarine
225 g (8 oz) sieved icing sugar
a few drops peppermint essence

TO SERVE
paper fairy-cake cases

1. Put the egg white into a medium-sized mixing bowl and agitate with a wooden spoon until frothy (as though you were going to make royal icing).
2. Gradually stir in the icing sugar until a really stiff fondant results. The consistency should be rather like marzipan, and you will have to end up kneading the last bit of icing sugar in with your hands.
3. Roll the mixture into 20 small, even-sized balls, each about the size of a marble.
4. Arrange 6 balls in a ring fashion on a lightly greased large flat dinner plate.
5. Microwave for 1½ minutes on 100%/HIGH – the meringues will puff up dramatically and become firm very quickly.
6. Set aside to stand, and repeat until all the mixture has been used up.
7. Transfer to cooling tray and allow to cool.
8. Meanwhile, make the butter cream. Put the margarine into a medium-sized mixing bowl and microwave on 100%/HIGH for 10 seconds.
9. Gradually beat in the sieved icing sugar, using a wooden spoon. Beat in the peppermint essence to taste.
10. Sandwich the meringue halves together with the prepared butter cream and serve in paper cases.

PINEAPPLE UPSIDE-DOWN PUDDING

Chocolate pudding with pineapple – a delicious combination. This rich chocolate pudding microwaves extremely well and makes an attractive dessert that is delicious hot or cold. Serve with reduced-fat single cream or ice cream.

PREPARATION TIME: 17 minutes
MICROWAVE COOKING TIME: 6–7 minutes
SERVES: 4

227 g (8 oz) can pineapple slices in natural juice
115 g (4 oz) polyunsaturated margarine, soft
115 g (4 oz) soft dark brown sugar
85 g (3 oz) self-raising flour } sieved
30 g (1 oz) cocoa powder } together
2 eggs, size 3

1. Lightly grease an 18 cm (7″) soufflé dish with margarine. Reserving 1 tbsp juice, drain the pineapple slices well and arrange in an attractive pattern on the base of the dish.
2. In a large bowl combine the margarine, sugar, flour and cocoa, eggs and pineapple juice. Beat for about 1 minute with a wooden spoon.
3. Turn mixture on to prepared pineapple slices.
4. Microwave, uncovered, on 100%/HIGH for 6–7 minutes. Turn the pudding half a turn twice during cooking.
5. Allow to stand in container for 10 minutes, then turn out with the pineapple on top, and serve hot or cold.

NOTE: For dinner parties cook this pudding in advance and turn it out on to an attractive plate. Just before serving pour a little kirsch over the pud and re-heat for about 3 minutes on 100%/HIGH. No need to cover – tastes wonderful!

CHOCOLATE GÂTEAU

Chocolate and raspberries combine well in this beautifully moist gâteau. The filling is made from low-fat soft cheese, honey and orange rind. The cake is finished with chocolate glacé icing and decorated with fresh raspberries.

PREPARATION TIME: 15 minutes
MICROWAVE COOKING TIME: 14 minutes
MAKES: 8 slices

FOR THE CAKE
115 g (4 oz) polyunsaturated margarine
115 g (4 oz) soft dark brown sugar
4 eggs, size 3, beaten
225 g (8 oz) self-raising wholemeal flour
30 g (1 oz) cocoa
1 tsp baking powder } **sieved together**
3 tbsp milk

FOR THE FILLING
170 g (6 oz) Quark low-fat soft cheese
1 tbsp set honey
grated rind of ½ orange
1–2 tbsp semi-skimmed milk

FOR THE ICING
170 g (6 oz) icing sugar
1 tbsp cocoa } **sieved together**
about 3 tbsp boiling water
15 g (½ oz) margarine
grated rind of ½ orange

TO DECORATE
a few fresh raspberries

1. Lightly grease a deep, 20 cm (8″) microwave ring mould and line the base with a ring of greaseproof paper.
2. To prepare the cake, beat together the margarine and sugar until light and fluffy. Beat in the eggs gradually.
3. Gradually fold in the flour mixture with the milk.
4. Spoon the mixture into the prepared container. Even out the surface.

5. Microwave, uncovered, on 40%/SIMMER for about 14 minutes, turning the container half a turn 2–3 times during cooking. Allow to stand for 10 minutes.
6. Turn out on to a wire cooling rack, on which has been placed 2 sheets of absorbent kitchen paper, sprinkled with a little castor sugar. Allow to become quite cold.
7. Cut the cake in half horizontally and put one half on a serving dish.
8. Prepare the filling. Beat together the low-fat soft cheese, honey, orange rind and milk until well combined and creamy. Spread this mixture over cake on serving dish. Top with other half of cake.
9. Make the icing. Put the sieved icing sugar and cocoa into a mixing bowl and beat to a smooth consistency with the boiling water. Beat in margarine and grated orange rind.
10. Quickly spread the glacé icing over the cake evenly.
11. Decorate with the fresh raspberries and serve immediately.

GROUND ALMOND SHORTBREAD

Shortbread is traditionally from Scotland, where it is eaten all the year round, but it is particularly associated with Hogmanay or New Year. The microwave lends itself well to the cooking of shortbread, as it should be served a nice, pale colour, sprinkled with a little castor sugar. Be careful not to overcook, or the shortbread will have brown patches inside.

PREPARATION TIME: 15 minutes
MICROWAVE COOKING TIME: 7½–9 minutes
MAKES: 6–8 pieces

170 g (6 oz) polyunsaturated margarine, cold from fridge
85 g (3 oz) soft light brown sugar
255 g (9 oz) plain flour, sieved
30 g (1 oz) almond nibs
a few drops of almond essence

TO SERVE
castor sugar, for sprinkling

1. Lightly grease an 18 cm (7″) flan dish with a little margarine.
2. Combine the chilled margarine and sugar, using the hands, until well mixed. Gradually work in the flour, almond nibs and almond essence to form a pliable dough.
3. Press the dough into the greased flan dish, again using your hands.
4. Prick all over with a fork. Refrigerate for 15 minutes.
5. Microwave, uncovered, on 70%/ROAST for 7½–9 minutes giving the dish half a turn twice during cooking.
6. Remove from microwave and allow to cool in container for 15 minutes.
7. Cut into fingers and serve when quite cold, sprinkled with a little castor sugar.

RICH FRUIT CAKE

I often use this recipe for my Christmas cake, as it is quick and simple to cook, yet stays beautifully moist. Just as with conventionally made Christmas cake, I ensure it is well spiked with sherry or brandy in the weeks before it is iced. Prepare and cook one month before Christmas. Keep in an airtight container.

PREPARATION TIME: 20 minutes
MICROWAVE COOKING TIME: 35–40 minutes
MAKES: 8 slices

115 g (4 oz) polyunsaturated margarine
85 g (3 oz) dark soft brown sugar
2 tbsp black treacle
3 eggs, size 3
4 tbsp milk
225 g (8 oz) wholemeal self-raising flour } sieved
1 tsp mixed spice } together
55 g (2 oz) dried apricots, chopped
170 g (6 oz) raisins
170 g (6 oz) sultanas
115 g (4 oz) currants
115 g (4 oz) glacé cherries, washed and chopped
55 g (2 oz) hazelnuts, chopped

1. Lightly grease and line the base of a fairly deep 20 cm (8″) soufflé dish.
2. Cream the margarine, sugar and treacle until light and fluffy.
3. Beat in the eggs one at a time, adding a tablespoon of flour with each egg to stop the mixture curdling.
4. Beat in the milk.
5. Gradually fold in the flour and spice together with all the dried fruit and nuts.
6. Turn the mixture into the prepared soufflé dish and level the surface. Make a slight indent in the centre with the back of a spoon.
7. Microwave on 40%/SIMMER for 35–40 minutes. Allow to stand in container for 20 minutes before turning out.
8. When quite cold, cover with marzipan and icing, as for a traditional Christmas cake.

COMBINATION COOKING

- Toad-in-the-hole
- Roast beef
- Chicken and ham pie
- Cheese and onion plait
- Roast duck
- Egg and bacon flan with spinach
- Potato and onion layer
- Minced beef and potato pie
- Picnic sausage-meat pie
- Jacket potatoes with chicken and soured cream
- Barbecued chicken drumsticks
- Roast chicken with roast potatoes
- Savoury fish puffs
- Minced pork pie
- Strawberry choux ring
- Victoria sandwich
- Apple sponge pudding
- Cheese and onion soufflé
- Coffee and walnut éclairs
- Roast chicken with rice and marmalade stuffing
- Lancashire hot pot

Combination microwave ovens are fast becoming extremely popular, probably because they give you the crisp brown results you expect from your conventional oven in about one-third of the conventional cooking time. This high-speed cooking is achieved by combining microwave energy with hot-air cooking.

Combination ovens vary slightly from manufacturer to manufacturer, but, basically, the food is put into a cold oven and the oven is set according to the recipe. The cooker then starts to operate, and as the microwave energy reaches the heart of the food, the hot air oven reaches a high, pre-selected temperature very rapidly and this crisps and browns your food. The results are excellent.

You can use this kind of cooker, in three different ways; as a microwave oven, as a fan-assisted oven, or as a combination oven using both these facilities. Some manufacturers also incorporate a grill.

The recipes given in this section were tested in a Brother MF2100 high-speed cooker. Comparable results may be obtained in a Belling Triplette 343 and in a Bejam 801.

A NOTE ABOUT CONTAINERS FOR COMBINATION OVENS

All types of metal, non-stick or otherwise, may be used in these cookers when using COMBI or TURBO mode, but remember to place the insulating mat, if provided, in your cooker between the wire rack and the baking tin. Prepare the tins exactly as for conventional baking. Ovenproof glass, ceramic dishes and earthenware containers are also ideal. However, do ensure that dishes used for microwave cooking have no metal trim or content. Plastic containers specifically designed for microwave ovens are now widely available, but follow manufacturers' instructions closely, as some dishes are suitable for use with combination settings while less durable plastics are suitable only when the cooker is set for microwave alone.

The cooking time given at the beginning of each recipe does not always represent the total cooking time: some recipes use the microwave facility followed by combination cooking.

TOAD-IN-THE-HOLE

Use low-fat, preservative-free sausages for a healthier toad-in-the-hole. This recipe crisps to perfection in just 20 minutes, with no pre-heating, using the combination method. A quick and successful way to cook this popular traditional recipe.

PREPARATION TIME: 10 minutes
COMBINATION COOKING TIME: 20 minutes
SERVES: 4

450 g (1 lb) low-fat sausages or 450 g (1 lb) pork sausages
115 g (4 oz) plain flour
a little salt
2 eggs, size 2
285 ml (½ pt) semi-skimmed milk

1. Lightly grease a shallow dish and arrange the pricked sausages in a single layer over the base. A 25.5 cm (10″) pottery quiche dish is ideal for this recipe.
2. Sieve the flour into a large bowl. Add salt.
3. Make a well in the centre of the flour.
4. Beat together the eggs and milk and add to the flour a little at a time, beating with a wooden spoon or wire balloon whisk until a smooth batter results.
5. Pour the batter over the sausages and place the dish on the wire rack in the cooker.
6. Set the cooker on HIGH SPEED 250°C for 20 minutes.

NOTE: The toad-in-the-hole is cooked when it is well risen and looks crisp and brown.

If using a metal container, use insulating mat where applicable.

ROAST BEEF

Traditional roast beef with a crisp outer surface can be cooked to perfection in one-third to half the time it would take to cook conventionally. The juices are collected in the covered turntable and may be used to make gravy. As the juices are held in a microwave-free zone, the amount of splashing in the oven is kept to a minimum.

PREPARATION TIME: 5 minutes
COMBINATION COOKING TIME: 44 minutes
SERVES: 6

The beef will be cooked to a medium condition.
1.8 kg (4 lb) piece topside, taken from refrigerator
2 cloves garlic, cut into slithers

1. Using a sharp knife, make slits all over the joint and insert a slither of garlic in each one.
2. Arrange the splash trivet on the turntable in the oven, and place the joint on the trivet.
3. Set the cooker on HIGH SPEED 200°C for 44 minutes.
4. Turn the meat over once, halfway through the cooking time.
5. At the end of the cooking time, remove joint from oven and allow to stand for 10 minutes before carving.

NOTE: Use the juices collected under the splash trivet to make gravy, using the microwave facility.

CHICKEN AND HAM PIE

This traditional chicken pie uses cold chicken and ham with a light sauce. The shortcrust pastry is made with vegetable margarine and cooks perfectly in 14 minutes – no pre-heating either! Remember to use the insulating mat where provided, if using a metal baking tin. This recipe uses both the microwave and combination cooking facilities.

PREPARATION TIME: 30 minutes
COMBINATION COOKING TIME: 13 minutes
SERVES: 4

225 g (8 oz) cold, cooked chicken, roughly chopped
198 g (7 oz) can ham, roughly chopped

FOR THE SAUCE
1 onion, peeled and chopped
45 g (1½ oz) margarine
45 g (1½ oz) plain flour
salt and freshly ground black pepper
285 ml (½ pt) light chicken stock, hot
55 g (2 oz) frozen peas

FOR THE PASTRY CRUST
170 g (6 oz) plain flour, sieved
85 g (3 oz) polyunsaturated margarine, cold from fridge
beaten egg for brushing

1. Combine chicken and ham and place in the base of a 19 cm (7½″) round pie dish.
2. Put the onion into a cereal bowl. Cover and microwave on 100%/HIGH for 2 minutes. Stir and set aside.
3. Make the sauce. Put the margarine into a litre (2 pt) jug and microwave on 100%/HIGH for 30 seconds, or until melted and hot.
4. Stir in the flour. Gradually add the stock, stirring continuously.
5. Microwave, uncovered, on 100%/HIGH for 2 minutes, beating with a wire balloon whisk once or twice. The sauce will rise up in the jug and thicken.
6. Gently stir the peas and onion into the sauce. Season.
7. Pour sauce over the mixed meats and mix gently.
8. Make the pastry. Put the sieved flour into a large mixing bowl. Add the margarine, straight from the fridge, cut into pieces. Rub in until the mixture resembles fine breadcrumbs.
9. Mix to a dough, using cold water.
10. Knead lightly on a floured pastry board, then roll out to a circle a little larger than the pie dish, to make a lid.

11. From the outside edge of the pastry cut a strip to fit around the rim of the pie dish. Dampen the edge of the pie plate and lift the pastry strip on to it. Dampen the pastry strip.
12. Lift the 'lid' on to the pastry strip. Seal edges. Knock up and flute edge.
13. Use any left-over pastry to make leaves for decoration. Apply these to the pie, dampening with a little cold water first.
14. Make a hole in the pastry lid to allow steam to escape, then brush all over the pie with beaten egg.
15. Place the pie on a wire rack in the cooker. Set the cooker on HIGH SPEED 250°C and cook for 13 minutes. The pastry will be crisp and golden. Serve immediately.

CHEESE AND ONION PLAIT

Low-fat cheese and onion mixed with a little beaten egg makes a delicious low-fat filling for this pie, which uses packet puff pastry for convenience. This pie is delicious hot, but is also useful cold and may be served on the buffet table or taken on picnics.

PREPARATION TIME: 30 minutes
COMBINATION COOKING TIME: 15 minutes
SERVES: 6

1 medium onion, chopped
340 g (12 oz) packet puff pastry, thawed if frozen
1 egg, size 2, beaten
1 tsp dried oregano
170 g (6 oz) low-fat Cheddar-type cheese, grated

FOR THE TOPPING
30 g (1 oz) low-fat Cheddar-type cheese, grated
½ tsp oregano
1 tsp paprika pepper

1. Put the onion into a medium-sized bowl. Cover and microwave on 100%/HIGH for 2 minutes. Set aside.

2. Cut the pastry in half, then, on a floured board, roll each half into a 25 cm × 20 cm (10″ × 8″) rectangle.
3. Beat the egg with a fork and then add most of it to the onion. Reserve just enough to glaze the plait before baking.
4. Add oregano and grated cheese to onion and mix well.
5. Using a pastry brush and cold water, brush all round edge of one piece of pastry.
6. Spread cheese and onion mixture all over this half, coming almost up to the edge.
7. Fold remaining piece of pastry in half lengthways and cut slits with a sharp knife at ½″ intervals right down the length of this piece, from the fold to within ¼″ of edge.
8. Leave the piece folded and lift it on to the filled piece. Open out and press edges down to seal. Trim edges.
9. Knock up and flute edges. Lift on to insulating mat.
10. Brush top of plait all over with remaining beaten egg.
11. Combine all ingredients for topping and sprinkle over the plait evenly.
12. Position the insulating mat on the wire rack on the splash trivet in the cooker.
13. Cook on HIGH SPEED 250°C for 15 minutes.

NOTE: It is easy to lift the prepared plait on to the insulating mat if you use two fish slices.

ROAST DUCK

Roast duck gives a touch of excellence to any dinner party. In this recipe the duck is marinated before cooking and then cooked to crisp perfection using the combination oven. Serve with an orange salad.

PREPARATION TIME: 10 minutes plus marinating time
COMBINATION COOKING TIME: 27 minutes
SERVES: 4

1 duckling weighing 2 kg (4½ lb) (remove giblets and use for stock)

FOR THE MARINADE
2 tbsp soya sauce
3 tbsp red wine vinegar
1 tbsp olive oil
6 tbsp red wine
1 tsp soft light brown sugar
2 cloves garlic, crushed

1. Place the defrosted duck in any suitable large container, after removing giblets.
2. Mix all ingredients for the marinade and pour over the duck. Cover with clingfilm and refrigerate for at least 4 hours, or overnight. Baste duck with the mixture 3 or 4 times.
3. Lift duck from marinade and drain well.
4. Prick duck all over with a fork to help the fat run.
5. Arrange splash trivet on turntable. Arrange duck, breast side down, immediately on trivet.
6. Set the oven on HIGH SPEED 250°C for 27 minutes.
7. Halfway through cooking time, carefully turn the duck over so that it is breast side up and continue to cook for remainder of time.
8. Allow to stand for 10 minutes before carving.

EGG AND BACON FLAN WITH SPINACH

Egg and bacon flan was a very popular lunch for farm workers. It is filling, nutritious and can easily be packed to take out for the day. This recipe uses a low-fat cheese and semi-skimmed milk. Serve warm or cold.

PREPARATION TIME: 20 minutes
COMBINATION COOKING TIME: 16 minutes
SERVES: 6

225 g (8 oz) shortcrust pastry made with wholemeal flour and polyunsaturated margarine (see p. 137 for method)
6 eggs, size 3, with 1 separated
115 g (4 oz) frozen chopped spinach, defrosted
4 rashers lean streaky bacon, de-rinded and chopped
1 medium onion, peeled and chopped
225 ml (8 fl oz) semi-skimmed milk
salt and freshly ground black pepper
170 g (6 oz) low-fat Cheddar-type cheese grated

1. Roll the pastry out and use to line a 27 cm (10″) pottery flan dish. Prick the base lightly with a fork.
2. Brush the pastry case with the white of egg. Chill for 10 minutes.
3. Put the spinach into a sieve and squeeze out any excess water.
4. Put the bacon and onion into a small bowl. Cover and microwave on 100%/HIGH for 4 minutes. Stir halfway through and at end of cooking time. Drain on a double layer of kitchen paper.
5. Put the milk and eggs, including any remaining white, into a mixing bowl. Season. Beat lightly with a balloon whisk.
6. Sprinkle the drained bacon and onion evenly over the pastry case. Add the grated cheese.
7. Stir the drained spinach into the egg mixture. Pour into flan case.
8. Put flan into cooker on rack and cook on HIGH SPEED 250°C for 16 minutes.
9. Serve warm or cold.

POTATO AND ONION LAYER

Potatoes have a reasonable vitamin C content and this dish is crisp and delicious with its cheese and breadcrumb topping. An excellent supper dish, which is good served with grilled tomatoes and baked beans.

PREPARATION TIME: 15 minutes
COMBINATION COOKING TIME: 23 minutes
SERVES: 4

900 g (2 lb) old white potatoes, peeled and thinly sliced
2 medium onions, ringed
salt and freshly ground black pepper
8 tbsp semi-skimmed milk
30 g (1 oz) fresh breadcrumbs
55 g (2 oz) low-fat Cheddar-type cheese, grated

1. Soak the potato slices in cold water for 15–20 minutes to remove surface starch.
2. Put the onion rings into a medium-sized mixing bowl. Cover and microwave on 100%/HIGH for 3 minutes. Set aside.
3. Grease a 1.4 l (2½ pt) entrée dish. Layer the drained potatoes with the part-cooked onions in the dish, starting and ending with potato. Season each layer with a little salt and pepper.
4. Pour the milk over the potatoes.
5. Combine the breadcrumbs and cheese and sprinkle evenly over the surface of the dish.
6. Place the dish on the wire rack in the cooker and cook on HIGH SPEED 250°C for 23 minutes.
7. Allow to stand for 4 minutes before serving.

MINCED BEEF AND POTATO PIE

Choose lean minced beef, and semi-skimmed milk to make the sauce for this recipe. The cheese topping colours beautifully in the combination oven and this attractive meal, cooked in one pot, needs only a salad accompaniment to make it into a main meal.

PREPARATION TIME: 20 minutes
COMBINATION COOKING TIME: 25 minutes
SERVES: 4–6

680 g (1½ lb) old potatoes, scrubbed clean
1 rasher back bacon, de-rinded and chopped
1 medium onion, chopped
285 g (10 oz) lean minced beef
225 g (8 oz) chicken livers, membranes removed, chopped
1 ripe tomato, peeled and chopped
2 cloves garlic, chopped
salt and freshly ground black pepper

FOR THE SAUCE
45 g (1½ oz) polyunsaturated margarine
45 g (1½ oz) plain flour
1 tsp made mustard
425 ml (¾ pt) semi-skimmed milk
85 g (3 oz) grated low-fat Cheddar-type cheese

1. Slice the potatoes thinly and leave to soak in plenty of cold water for 15–20 minutes to remove surface starch.
2. Put the bacon and onion into a large casserole. Cover and then microwave on 100%/HIGH for 3 minutes. Stir in the minced beef and the chicken livers. Stir well with a fork. Cover and microwave on 100%/HIGH for 5 minutes. Stir and re-cover after 3 minutes. Stir in the tomato and garlic, season and stir well again.
3. Turn the meat mixture out into a separate dish.
4. Drain the potatoes, then part cook them by putting them into a fairly large dish with 1 tbsp water. Cover and microwave on 100%/HIGH for 6 minutes. Set aside for 5 minutes.
5. Using a spoon and fork, carefully arrange half of the part-cooked potato slices over the base of the large casserole that the mince was cooked in. Top with the meat mixture. Cover with the remaining potatoes, discarding any liquid.
6. Make the sauce. Put the margarine into a litre (2 pt) jug and microwave on 100%/HIGH for 30–45 seconds, or until melted and hot.
7. Stir in the flour and mustard. Gradually blend in the milk.
8. Microwave, uncovered, on 100%/HIGH for 3½–5 minutes, until the sauce boils and thickens. Stir frequently with a balloon whisk. Gently fold in 55 g (2 oz) of the grated cheese.
9. Pour the sauce evenly over the prepared dish.
10. Sprinkle remaining cheese over the surface. Do not cover.

11. Place on the turntable in the cooker and cook on HIGH SPEED 250°C for 25 minutes.
12. Allow to stand for 5 minutes, then serve with a green vegetable or a mixed salad.

PICNIC SAUSAGE-MEAT PIE

Puff pastry is particularly good cooked in a combination oven. It rises in puffy flakes and cooks to golden perfection in about one-third of the time it would take normally. It is important to place the pie on the insulating mat and then place the mat on the wire rack. Serve this traditional pie, with a salad, either warm for supper or allow it to cool and pack it up for a picnic lunch.

PREPARATION TIME: 30 minutes
COMBINATION COOKING TIME: 19 minutes
SERVES: 6–8

450 g (1 lb) good quality pork sausage-meat
225 g (8 oz) chicken livers, membranes removed, chopped
1 onion, finely chopped
2 tsp dried mixed herbs
450 g (1 lb) Baxters' fresh puff pastry, free from animal fat
a little beaten egg to glaze

1. Combine sausage-meat, chicken livers, onion and herbs. Mix well and form into a brick shape using floured hands.
2. Roll out pastry into a rectangle, about 30 cm × 25 cm (12″ × 10″) – a piece that will be large enough to completely enclose the sausage-meat 'brick'.
3. Lift sausage-meat into centre of pastry. Brush edges with water. Fold over the pastry to meet in centre, tucking in the ends.
4. Arrange pie on insulating mat, placing the fold underneath.
5. Brush all over with beaten egg. Use left-over pastry to make pastry leaves. Arrange these attractively on pie and glaze with beaten egg.
6. Make 3 slits in centre of pie to allow steam to escape.

7. Place pie on insulating mat, then place both on wire rack in cooker.
8. Cook on HIGH SPEED 250°C for 19 minutes. Serve warm or cold with salad.

JACKET POTATOES WITH CHICKEN AND SOURED CREAM

Jacket potatoes with crisp outer skins have been popular for centuries. Potatoes have a reasonable vitamin C content and are high in fibre while fairly low in calories. Most people know that the microwave oven cooks a jacket potato in about 5 minutes, but they are often very disappointed with the soft skin. Combination cooking means fast jacket potatoes with lovely crisp skins – accompanied by a mixed salad, what could be a better supper dish?

PREPARATION TIME: 15 minutes
COMBINATION COOKING TIME: 29 minutes
SERVES: 4 as a main meal, 8 as a snack

4 large baking potatoes, about 225 g (8 oz) each
2 spring onions, chopped
170 g (6 oz) chopped, cooked chicken
140 ml (5 fl oz) soured cream
salt and freshly ground black pepper
grated Parmesan cheese for sprinkling

1. Wash and dry the potatoes, then prick each one in 2 or 3 places with a fork.
2. Place on wire rack in the cooker and cook on HIGH SPEED 250°C for 24 minutes.
3. Allow to stand for 5 minutes, then, using oven gloves, cut each potato in half horizontally from end to end.
4. Scoop out the potato flesh and turn into a mixing bowl. Mash down well. Add spring onions, chopped chicken and soured cream. Mix well, seasoning to taste.

5. Divide the prepared filling between the potato halves and arrange them in a ring on a serving dish.
6. Sprinkle with grated Parmesan.
7. Put the serving dish on to the wire rack and cook on HIGH SPEED 250°C for 5 mins. Serve immediately with a mixed salad.

BARBECUED CHICKEN DRUMSTICKS

Chicken cooked until tender in a delicious barbecue sauce will be spicy and beautifully brown when cooked in a combination oven. Serve these popular drumsticks on a bed of rice with a crisp green side salad.

PREPARATION TIME: 10 minutes plus marinating time
MICROWAVE COOKING TIME: 20 minutes
SERVES: 4

8 chicken drumsticks

FOR THE BARBECUE SAUCE
1 tbsp vegetable oil
1 onion, finely chopped
2 tbsp tomato purée
2 tbsp clear honey
2 tbsp soya sauce
1 tbsp paprika
1 tsp mild curry powder
3 tbsp water
1 tbsp freshly chopped parsley

1. Make the sauce. Place oil and onions in a medium-sized mixing bowl. Cover and microwave on 100%/HIGH for 2 minutes. Stir in all remaining ingredients.
2. Arrange chicken drumsticks in suitable shallow dish.
3. Pierce each one several times with a sharp knife.
4. Spoon the sauce over the drumsticks. Cover.
5. Leave to marinate for 1 hour, turning the drumsticks in the sauce once or twice.

6. Remove cover. Place dish on wire rack and cook on HIGH SPEED 250°C for 20 minutes.

ROAST CHICKEN WITH ROAST POTATOES

Combination cooking means chicken with a lovely crisp skin which is tender and full of flavour, cooked together with crisp and golden roast potatoes. A wonderfully quick way to cook the traditional Sunday roast.

PREPARATION TIME: 15 minutes
COMBINATION COOKING TIME: 32–40 minutes*
SERVES: 4

1 × 1.8 kg (4 lb) fresh roasting chicken (remove giblets and use for gravy)
680 g (1½ lb) potatoes, peeled and cut as for conventional roasting
vegetable oil
a little salt

1. Place the trivet in place on the turntable. Arrange the prepared potatoes on the trivet and brush with vegetable oil. Sprinkle with a little salt.
2. Cook on HIGH SPEED 250°C for 7 minutes.
3. Tie legs of chicken together with string. Brush the chicken all over with oil, then lift it on to the wire rack. Mask wings with 2 small strips of foil. Place it in the cooker, above the potatoes.
4. Cook on HIGH SPEED 250°C for 20 minutes, then turn the bird over for the remainder of the calculated cooking time. Allow the chicken to stand for 10 minutes before carving.

*To calculate cooking time, weigh the bird before brushing with oil and allow 8–10 minutes per 450 g (1 lb). Remember there is no need to pre-heat the combination oven.

NOTE: Large birds will need to be placed on the drip tray as there will not be room for both rack and bird.

SAVOURY FISH PUFFS

Pastry has formed an important part of the traditional British menu for centuries. Choux pastry is lighter than shortcrust or puff pastry, both of which contain larger quantities of fat. This recipe uses polyunsaturated margarine in the choux pastry and the sauce is made from semi-skimmed milk or stock, with cod, peas and low-fat cheese. A healthy approach to pastry. Serve with coleslaw and a tomato salad.

PREPARATION TIME: 20 minutes
COMBINATION COOKING TIME: 14 minutes
SERVES: 4 (makes 12 fairly large puffs)

FOR THE FISH SAUCE
225 g (8 oz) piece filleted cod
285 ml (½ pt) semi-skimmed milk or fish stock
salt and freshly ground black pepper
45 g (1½ oz) polyunsaturated margarine
45 g (1½ oz) plain flour
55 g (2 oz) low-fat Cheddar-type cheese
55 g (2 oz) frozen peas
1 tbsp freshly chopped parsley

FOR THE CHOUX PASTRY
55 g (2 oz) polyunsaturated margarine
70 g (2½ oz) plain flour, sieved
2 eggs, size 3 beaten

1. Arrange fish in a shallow dish. Add 1 tbsp milk or stock and season. Cover and microwave on 100%/HIGH for 2½ minutes. Set aside.
2. Make the sauce. Put the margarine into a litre (2 pt) jug and microwave on 100%/HIGH for about 45 seconds, or until melted and hot.
3. Stir in the flour. Season.
4. Measure the liquid resulting from the cooked fish and make it up to 285 ml (½ pt) with the stock or milk.
5. Gradually stir this liquid into the roux mixture in the jug.

Microwave on 100%/HIGH for 3–4 minutes, stirring every minute with a balloon whisk.
6. Stir in cheese, frozen peas and parsley. Flake fish and add to sauce.
7. Make the choux pastry. Put 140 ml (5 fl oz) water and the margarine into a medium-sized mixing bowl and microwave on 100%/HIGH for 3–4 minutes, or until the water boils and the margarine melts.
8. Add the flour all in one go and beat thoroughly with a wooden spoon until a smooth ball of dough forms. Allow to cool slightly.
9. Gradually beat in the beaten eggs a little at a time until the mixture is smooth and shiny.
10. Remove turntable from cooker, grease it lightly, then put teaspoonfuls of the choux paste directly on to turntable.
11. Put turntable into cooker. Cook on HIGH SPEED 250°C for 14 minutes, or until the pastry balls are well puffed up and golden.
12. Transfer to cooling tray. Immediately slit each puff with a sharp knife to allow steam to escape.
13. To serve, fill each puff with some of the prepared fish sauce and arrange on a serving dish. Pour remaining sauce into centre of dish and serve immediately.

MINCED PORK PIE

So often shepherd's pie is made from inferior, fatty meat, which cooks down to a gristly, tasteless mass. This version made from minced pork cooked with herbs and vegetables and topped with creamy potatoes is a delicious improvement on tradition.

PREPARATION TIME: 15 minutes
COMBINATION COOKING TIME: 10 minutes
SERVES: 4

FOR THE POTATO TOPPING
680 g (1½ lb) old potatoes, peeled
3 tbsp semi-skimmed milk
15 g (½ oz) butter
extra milk for mashing
salt and freshly ground black pepper
30 g (1 oz) low-fat Cheddar-type cheese, grated

FOR THE MINCE BASE
1 large onion, chopped
1 clove garlic, chopped
1 carrot, peeled and diced
450 g (1 lb) minced pork
1 tsp dried mixed herbs
1 tbsp tomato purée
227 g (8 oz) can chopped tomatoes
salt and freshly ground black pepper

1. Prepare the potato topping. Dice the prepared potatoes and put them into a large casserole or 1.7 l (3 pt) mixing bowl. Add the milk.
2. Cover and microwave on 100%/HIGH for 12 minutes.
3. Stir, re-cover and set aside for 5 minutes.
4. Prepare the mince base. Put the onion, garlic and carrot into a 1.1 l (2 pt) pie dish. Cover and microwave on 100%/HIGH for 3 minutes. Stir in the pork. Cover and microwave on 100%/HIGH for 5 minutes. Pour off excess liquid.
5. Stir in the herbs, tomato purée and the chopped tomatoes with any juices. Mix well. Season.
6. Cover and microwave on 50%/MEDIUM for 10 minutes.
7. Meanwhile mash down the potatoes, adding butter, extra milk and seasoning.
8. Top the meat mixture with the mashed potato. Make pattern with fork.
9. Sprinkle with the grated cheese.
10. Place the pie on the wire rack in the cooker and cook on HIGH SPEED 250°C for 10 minutes.

STRAWBERRY CHOUX RING

This delightful choux ring is one of my favourite summer desserts. The filling is a delicious combination of Greek yoghurt and cream with fresh strawberries. Covered with a 'snow' of icing sugar, this dessert is appealing to the eye and very good to eat.

PREPARATION TIME: 15 minutes
COMBINATION COOKING TIME: 14 minutes
SERVES: 6

FOR THE CHOUX PASTRY
make exactly as given for savoury fish puffs on page 148

FOR THE FILLING
142 ml (5 fl oz) carton double cream
142 ml (5 fl oz) carton Greek yoghurt
2 tbsp clear honey
225 g (8 oz) fresh strawberries, hulled
sifted icing sugar for dredging

1. Put the choux pastry into a piping bag fitted with a 1.25 cm (½″) plain tube.
2. Lightly grease the turntable and pipe a circle of choux pastry round the edge.
3. Put the turntable into the cooker.
4. Cook on HIGH SPEED 250°C for 14 minutes.
5. Transfer to cooling rack and make slits with a sharp knife to allow steam to escape.
6. When cool, transfer to serving dish.
7. Prepare the filling. Whip the cream until it holds its shape, then fold it into the yoghurt. Stir in the honey.
8. Reserve 2 evenly sized strawberries for decoration, slice remainder and fold into yoghurt and cream.
9. Just before serving, cut choux ring in half horizontally. Carefully lift off the lid.
10. Fill the cavity with the prepared filling. Replace top and sprinkle with a snow of sifted icing sugar. Decorate with reserved strawberries, cut as desired.

VICTORIA SANDWICH

As explained in the baking section, where a recipe is given for a microwave Victoria sandwich, this particular cake was made very popular in England by Queen Victoria, who often asked that one be baked for Albert. She would have been amazed at the speed at which this one is successfully baked, especially as the mixture is put into a cold oven.

PREPARATION TIME: 15 minutes
COMBINATION COOKING TIME: 11 minutes
MAKES: 6–8 slices

170 g (6 oz) polyunsaturated margarine
170 g (6 oz) castor sugar
½ tsp vanilla essence
3 eggs, size 2, beaten
170 g (6 oz) self-raising flour } sieved
½ tsp baking powder } together
2–3 tbsp reduced-sugar fruits of the forest jam

1. Lightly grease and line 2 × 20 cm (8″) sandwich tins.
2. Put the margarine and castor sugar into a mixing bowl and microwave on 100%/HIGH for 10–13 seconds, or until margarine is soft.
3. Add vanilla essence, beaten eggs and sifted flour and baking powder.
4. Using a wooden spoon, mix ingredients to combine then beat for 1 minute.
5. Divide prepared mixture between the tins. Level the surfaces.
6. Put one tin directly on centre of turntable and the other on the insulating mat, which has been placed on the wire rack above.
7. Cook on HIGH SPEED 250°C for 11 minutes. The top cake should be removed after 8 minutes' cooking; the rack should also be removed and the lower cake left to continue cooking for the remaining 3 minutes.

8. Turn out on to wire cooling rack and allow to cool.
9. When cold, spread one half with jam. Top with remaining half and serve.

APPLE SPONGE PUDDING

This delicious dessert crisps and browns when cooked in a combination microwave oven. A quick and easy family pudding, particularly good in the autumn when the apples have come from the garden.

PREPARATION TIME: 15 minutes
COMBINATION COOKING TIME: 10 minutes
SERVES: 4

450 g (1 lb) Bramley's cooking apples, cored, peeled and sliced
55 g (2 oz) demerara sugar

FOR THE SPONGE
55 g (2 oz) polyunsaturated margarine, at room temperature
55 g (2 oz) castor sugar
85 g (3 oz) self-raising flour
1 egg, size 2, beaten
1 tbsp milk

1. Put the apples and demerara sugar in layers in the bottom of an 850 ml (1½ pt) ovenproof pudding basin.
2. Put all the ingredients for the sponge into a mixing bowl and, using a wooden spoon, mix until combined then beat well for about 1 minute.
3. Cover the fruit evenly with the prepared sponge mixture.
4. Place on the rack in the cooker. Cook on HIGH SPEED 250°C for 10 minutes.

NOTE: Don't worry that the sponge mixture comes almost to the top of the pudding basin when it is added. The apple drops as it cooks and the sponge encloses the apple, resulting in a perfect apple sponge with a crisp gold top.

CHEESE AND ONION SOUFFLÉ

Soufflé is originally French, but it became popular and widely used in this country from the mid-nineteenth century. Many variations are now served, cheese soufflé being one of the easiest, as the cooking dish needs no special preparation. Serve with jacket potatoes and a salad.

PREPARATION TIME: 10 minutes
COMBINATION COOKING TIME: 15 minutes
SERVES: 3

1 medium onion, chopped
55 g (2 oz) polyunsaturated margarine
45 g (1½ oz) plain flour
285 ml (½ pt) semi-skimmed milk
salt and freshly ground black pepper
140 g (5 oz) mature Cheddar cheese, grated
½ tsp made English mustard
4 eggs, size 2, separated

1. Put the onion into a small dish.
2. Cover and microwave on 100%/HIGH for 2 minutes. Set aside.
3. Put the margarine into a 1.7 l (3 pt) mixing bowl. Microwave, uncovered, on 100%/HIGH for 1½ minutes, or until melted and hot. Stir in the flour. Mix well. Gradually blend in the milk, stirring. Season.
4. Microwave, uncovered, for 4–5 minutes, or until boiling and thickened. Beat with a balloon whisk every minute.
5. Stir in the cheese until it melts, then add the mustard and cooked onion.
6. Beat the yolks one at a time into the sauce.
7. Whisk the egg whites in a clean bowl until they stand in soft peaks. Fold the beaten egg whites into the sauce.
8. Lightly grease a 1.7 l (3 pt) soufflé dish.
9. Spoon the soufflé mixture lightly into the dish.
10. Arrange the soufflé dish on the rack in the cooker.
11. Cook on HIGH SPEED 250°C for 14–15 minutes, or until well risen, golden brown and set. Serve immediately.

COFFEE AND WALNUT ECLAIRS

Originally borrowed from the French, éclairs are now very popular in this country, served with afternoon tea or as an after-dinner dessert. They freeze well and are a wonderful standby to have in the freezer as they defrost quickly. They are best defrosted at room temperature rather than in the microwave.

PREPARATION TIME: 15 minutes
COMBINATION COOKING TIME: 14 minutes
MAKES: 19 éclairs

FOR THE CHOUX PASTRY
make exactly as given for savoury fish puffs on page 148

FOR THE FILLING
140 ml (5 fl oz) half-fat double cream
1 tsp coffee essence
30 g (1 oz) walnuts, finely chopped

FOR THE GLACÉ ICING
225 g (8 oz) icing sugar
¾ tsp instant coffee granules diluted with about 2 tbsp boiling water
30 g (1 oz) polyunsaturated margarine

1. Put the choux pastry into a piping bag fitted with a 1.25 cm (½″) plain tube.
2. Lightly grease the turntable and pipe out éclairs, each about 3 cm (1½″) long. Leave enough space for the éclairs to expand on rising.
3. Put the turntable into the oven and cook on HIGH SPEED 250°C for 14 minutes.
4. Transfer to cooling rack. Immediately split each éclair with a sharp knife to allow steam to escape. Allow to cool.
5. Whip the cream until it stands in soft peaks. Fold in finely chopped walnuts and coffee essence.
6. Fill a clean piping bag, fitted with a small plain tube, with the walnut and cream mixture. Divide cream evenly between éclairs.

7. To make the icing, sift icing sugar into a bowl.
8. Dilute the coffee granules with the boiling water, stirring well. Gradually mix this into the icing sugar to make a smooth icing. Beat in the margarine, which will give the icing a good gloss.
9. Holding each éclair carefully, dip them individually, upside-down, into the icing. Place immediately into paper fairy-cake cases.
10. Allow icing to set, then serve as soon as possible.

ROAST CHICKEN WITH RICE AND MARMALADE STUFFING

Corn-fed fresh chicken stuffed with a wonderful mixture of cooked brown rice, onion, marmalade and mushrooms. The bird is then brushed with olive oil and sprinkled with herbs before being roasted to golden perfection using the combination setting. The chicken will cook in about half the time it would take if cooked conventionally.

PREPARATION TIME: 15 minutes
COMBINATION COOKING TIME: 32–40 minutes*
SERVES: 6

1 × 1.8 kg (4 lb) corn-fed fresh chicken (remove giblets and use for gravy)
1 tbsp olive oil
1 tsp mixed herbs
½ tsp paprika

FOR THE STUFFING
1 medium onion, chopped
2 tbsp marmalade
85 g (3 oz) chopped button mushrooms
2 tbsp cooked brown rice
1 tsp dried parsley
salt and freshly ground black pepper

1. Prepare the stuffing. Put the chopped onion into a 1.7 l (3 pt) casserole. Cover and microwave on 100%/HIGH for 2 min-

utes. Stir in the marmalade, chopped mushrooms, brown rice and the dried parsley. Stir well, seasoning lightly.

2. Use the stuffing to stuff the neck end of the bird. Truss using wooden cocktail sticks. Tie legs together with string and mask wings with two small strips of foil.
3. Brush the bird all over with the olive oil. Combine the mixed herbs and paprika and sprinkle over the bird.
4. Place the prepared bird, breast side down, on the rack, over the drip tray.
5. Cook on HIGH SPEED 250°C for 20 minutes.
6. Turn the bird over and continue to microwave on HIGH SPEED 250°C for a further 18 minutes, or until cooked.
7. Allow to stand for 10 minutes, then serve.

*To calculate time, weigh the stuffed bird before brushing with oil and allow 8–10 minutes per 450 g (1 lb). Remember there is no pre-heating of the oven needed with a combination oven.

NOTE: Large birds will need to be placed directly on to the drip tray as there will not be room for the rack and the bird.

LANCASHIRE HOT POT

Lancashire hot pot was traditionally cooked in the bread oven after the loaves had been baked. It was considered an ideal filling meal for farm labourers returning from a busy day in the fields. This version cooks well in the combination oven. Serve with spring greens and carrots.

PREPARATION TIME: 30 minutes
COMBINATION COOKING TIME: 35 minutes
SERVES: 4

8 lean lamb loin chops
450 g (1 lb) onions, sliced
freshly ground black pepper
900 g (2 lb) potatoes, scrubbed clean and thickly sliced
285 ml (½ pt) good lamb or beef stock, hot

1. Brown chops on both sides in a little oil in your conventional frying-pan.
2. Layer the cutlets and onions into a large casserole (see note).
3. Season with black pepper.
4. Put the potato slices into another casserole. Add 1 tbsp water. Cover with a lid and microwave on 100%/HIGH for 6 minutes. Allow to stand for 5 minutes.
5. Using a spoon and fork, lift the drained part-cooked potato slices into the casserole containing the onions and chops. Arrange them so that they cover the cutlets and onions evenly.
6. Pour in stock.
7. Cover with a lid and cook on HIGH SPEED 250°C for 20 minutes, then remove lid and cook for a further 15 minutes, until potatoes and chops are tender.
8. Allow to stand for 10 minutes, then serve immediately.

NOTE: The large deep browning dish with a lid, MW10 made by Corning, is an ideal container for this recipe.

ENTERTAINING

Cod and salmon fish cakes
Ginger and apple fool
Glazed baked loin of pork
Vegetable and sausage risotto
Devilled kidneys
Wholemeal fruity suet pud
Braised shoulder of lamb with prunes
Beansprout stir-fry
Orange blancmange with Cointreau
Asparagus-stuffed chicken breasts
Rhubarb cheese
Beef rolls
Spicy meatballs
Minty mayonnaise sauce
Steak and kidney pudding
Wholefood Christmas pudding
Summer pudding
Veal, pork and spinach loaf
Lamb cobbler
Cream caramel

Entertaining friends in our own homes has been a popular social tradition for centuries. The microwave oven is definitely the one modern appliance that has made entertaining so much easier. Vegetables can be cooked quickly to perfection, they taste wonderful and look bright and colourful when presented. Many dinner party dishes may be cooked in advance and re-heated just before serving, leaving the hostess free to prepare herself and spend time with her guests immediately before the meal.

Desserts, custards and sauces may be cooked in between courses and the microwave can even be introduced as a source of entertainment: there's many a time I have made a chocolate pudding with a black cherry and kirsch topping or an upside-down pudding while the guests watched enthralled!

COD AND SALMON FISH CAKES

Fish cakes made of fresh cod combined with a little salmon and freshly mashed potatoes and flavoured with freshly chopped parsley are very different to the frozen variety with their bright orange breadcrumb coating.

These fish cakes are cooked quickly in the browning dish. Serve with a green salad and bread rolls. The salad should be tossed in a light garlic dressing.

PREPARATION TIME: 20 minutes
MICROWAVE COOKING TIME: 6 minutes plus pre-heating time
SERVES: 6

450 g (1 lb) fresh filleted cod, skinned and cut into 2.5 cm (1″) cubes
1 fillet salmon, about 115 g (4 oz), skinned
2 eggs, size 2, beaten
225 g (8 oz) freshly mashed potatoes (not too wet)
30 g (1 oz) fresh brown breadcrumbs
salt and freshly ground black pepper
1 tbsp freshly chopped parsley
1 clove garlic, chopped
2 tbsp oil

1. Put the cod into the food processor. Using the metal blade, process for a few seconds to chop finely.
2. Cut the salmon into small pieces and add it to the food processor with all other ingredients except the oil.
3. Process until well combined.
4. Shape into fish cakes.
5. Meanwhile pre-heat the large browning dish for 7 minutes on 100%/HIGH. Put the oil into the dish and microwave for 1½ minutes on 100%/HIGH.
6. Carefully lower the fish cakes into the hot oil.
7. Microwave, uncovered, on 100%/HIGH for 2½ minutes. Using a fish-slice, carefully turn each fish cake over and continue to microwave on 100%/HIGH for a further 2 minutes.
8. Drain well on absorbent kitchen paper before serving.

GINGER AND APPLE FOOL

In Elizabethan England, fools and flummeries were popular in this country. Today they are still served and provide a light dessert after a dinner or luncheon party. The crystallized ginger gives this Bramley fool a pleasant flavour.

PREPARATION TIME: 15 minutes
MICROWAVE COOKING TIME: 10 minutes
SERVES: 4

900 g (2 lb) Bramley's cooking apples, cored, peeled and sliced
4 tbsp castor sugar
¼ tsp ground nutmeg
285 ml (½ pt) half-fat double cream, whipped
crystallized ginger to taste

TO SERVE
1 green-skinned eating apple, cored, sliced and brushed liberally with lemon juice

1. Place the apple slices in a 2.3 l (4 pt) mixing bowl with the castor sugar and nutmeg.

2. Cover and microwave on 100%/HIGH for 10 minutes, stirring and re-covering after 5 minutes.
3. Stir and set aside, covered, until fairly cool.
4. Beat with a wooden spoon to a purée, then set aside until cold.
5. Fold the whipping cream and ginger into the apple purée. Turn into individual sundae dishes and refrigerate for at least one hour.
6. Serve each apple fool decorated with the slices of eating apple.

Glazed Baked Loin of Pork

Pork 'crackling' is not successful cooked in an ordinary microwave oven, so it is better to ask the butcher to remove this when he bones and rolls the joint for you. Take the skin home and roast it conventionally with the potatoes while you cook the joint in the microwave.

PREPARATION TIME: 10 minutes
MICROWAVE COOKING TIME: 41 minutes
SERVES: 6

1.8 kg (4 lb) piece of loin of pork, boned and rolled with skin removed

FOR THE GLAZE
1 tbsp tomato sauce
2 tsp soya sauce
1 tbsp freshly chopped parsley
½ tsp ground ginger

1. Mix all the ingredients for the glaze together and brush all over the meat.
2. Put the meat into a roasting bag and stand it on a microwave roasting rack, or, if no rack is available, arrange two saucers in the base of a large, shallow Pyrex dish and lift the joint on to them.

3. Microwave on 100%/HIGH for 11 minutes, then carefully turn the joint over and microwave on 70%/ROAST for 30 minutes.
4. Remove from microwave and slip the joint out of its roasting bag. Arrange on serving dish.
5. Cover the joint with a tent of foil and allow it to stand for 15 minutes before carving.

VEGETABLE AND SAUSAGE RISOTTO

Sausages were first made by the poor, who, wishing to use all parts of any animals they had killed, chopped the offal very finely and mixed it with fat, herbs, salt and spices. They then wrapped the ingredients in parts of the gut, and by so doing were able to preserve parts of the animal for a while.

This risotto is ideal for the microwave, as the whole meal is cooked in one pot, presenting a delicious and filling meal with very little washing-up.

PREPARATION TIME: 20 minutes
MICROWAVE COOKING TIME: 19 minutes
SERVES: 4

1 medium onion, chopped
1 medium red pepper, de-seeded and chopped
1 small cauliflower, florets only
550 ml (1 pt) boiling water or stock
225 g (8 oz) long-grain white rice
8 chipolata sausages, each cut into 3
225 g (8 oz) canned red kidney beans, drained and rinsed

TO SERVE
plenty of freshly chopped parsley

1. Put the onion, red pepper and cauliflower florets into a 2.3–2.8 l (4–5 pt) casserole.
2. Add 3 tbsp of stock or water.
3. Cover and microwave on 100%/HIGH for 5 minutes.

4. Stir in rice and remaining boiling water or stock.
5. Cover and microwave on 100%/HIGH for 14 minutes.
6. After 8 minutes' cooking time, stir in sausages.
7. Allow to stand, covered, for 5 minutes, then fork up, adding red kidney beans.
8. Serve immediately, sprinkled with plenty of freshly chopped parsley.

DEVILLED KIDNEYS

Kidneys, very popular as a breakfast dish with scrambled eggs, are now more often served as a lunch or supper dish. These devilled kidneys are delicious served on a bed of brown rice. Remember that kidneys do contain cholesterol, so they should not be served too often.

PREPARATION TIME: 20 minutes
MICROWAVE COOKING TIME: 9–10 minutes
SERVES: 3

10 lambs' kidneys, halved and cored

FOR THE MARINADE
2 tbsp corn oil
2 tbsp soya sauce
1 clove garlic, crushed
1 tbsp tomato sauce
2 tbsp dry sherry
½ tsp dried mixed herbs

1 tbsp corn oil
4 rashers back bacon, de-rinded and cut into strips
2 rounded tsp cornflour

1. Put the kidneys into a suitable shallow dish.
2. Mix all the ingredients for the marinade until well blended, then pour the marinade over the kidneys. Cover and refrigerate for at least 2 hours, or overnight if possible, turning the kidneys in the marinade frequently.

3. Put the oil into a casserole dish and microwave on 100%/HIGH for 1 minute.
4. Using a draining spoon, lift the kidneys into the heated oil. Add bacon strips. Cover and microwave on 100%/HIGH for 6–7 minutes, stirring and re-covering after 3 minutes.
5. Mix cornflour to a smooth paste with a little water and stir into kidneys. Microwave on 100%/HIGH for 2 minutes. Serve with rice.

WHOLEMEAL FRUITY SUET PUD

Suet puds should definitely be eaten only in moderation, but they do have a place on the British menu, especially on a very cold day and preferably after some vigorous exercise.

This is a light steamed pudding and is best served with a lemon sauce, ice-cream or Greek yoghurt.

PREPARATION TIME: 10 minutes
MICROWAVE COOKING TIME: 11 minutes
SERVES: 4

85 g (3 oz) self-raising wholemeal flour
85 g (3 oz) brown breadcrumbs
85 g (3 oz) shredded vegetable suet or polyunsaturated margarine
170 g (6 oz) dried mixed fruit, e.g. apricots, dates, raisins, chopped
1 tbsp clear honey
1 tbsp orange marmalade
1 egg, size 3, beaten
140 ml (¼ pt) pure orange juice, unsweetened

1. Mix all the ingredients together in a large bowl, starting with the dry ingredients, then adding the honey and marmalade, and then binding the mixture to a dough with the egg and orange juice.
2. Turn into a lightly greased 850 ml (1½ pt) pudding basin and microwave, covered, on 40%/SIMMER for about 9

minutes, then continue to microwave on 100%/HIGH for 2 minutes.

3. Allow to stand, covered, for 5 minutes, then turn out and serve hot.

BRAISED SHOULDER OF LAMB WITH PRUNES

Boiled mutton would have been far more usual in the seventeenth century, but as we very rarely buy mutton now, I have used shoulder of lamb in this recipe. Shoulder has a wonderful flavour, but do remove as much visible fat as possible before cooking. The joint may be studded with slithers cut from 3 cloves of garlic, if required.

PREPARATION TIME: 30 minutes
MICROWAVE COOKING TIME: 1 hour 10 minutes
SERVES: 6

1.5 kg (3½ lb) shoulder of lamb, all visible fat removed
2 rashers streaky bacon, rind removed, chopped
1 large onion, chopped
2 carrots, peeled and sliced
1 courgette, sliced
2 sticks celery, chopped
115 g (4 oz) dried prunes, no-need-to-soak type
½ tsp dried rosemary
300 ml (½ pt) stock, hot

FOR THE SAUCE
1 rounded tbsp cornflour
2 tbsp tomato purée

1. Melt down a little of the fat removed from the joint in a frying-pan on your conventional cooker.
2. Brown all the vegetables in the hot fat with the bacon. Drain well and transfer to a large casserole dish. Add prunes.
3. Brown joint in frying-pan. Drain well.
4. Top vegetables with the lamb. Add rosemary and stock.

5. Cover and microwave on 100%/HIGH for 10 minutes.
6. Continue to microwave on 40%/SIMMER for 1 hour, keeping the casserole covered throughout cooking time. Turn joint over after 20 minutes.
7. Allow to stand, covered, for 15 minutes, then arrange joint on serving dish, surrounded by the prunes and vegetables.
8. Strain the stock from the casserole into a large jug. Skim off any fat.
9. Cream the cornflour with a little water and stir into the stock with the tomato purée.
10. Microwave, uncovered, for about 3 minutes, or until sauce boils and thickens. Stir well.
11. Serve the lamb and hand the tomato sauce round separately.

BEANSPROUT STIR-FRY

Beansprouts are, of course, Chinese in origin and have only recently become popular in this country. They are rich in vitamins B and C and contain fibre, and they quickly turn a few boring ingredients into an exotic stir-fry.

PREPARATION TIME: 15 minutes
MICROWAVE COOKING TIME: 15 minutes
SERVES: 4

170 g (6 oz) button mushrooms, sliced
1 medium onion, finely chopped
1 clove garlic
170 g (6 oz) white cabbage, finely shredded
1 carrot, cut into matchsticks
55 g (2 oz) frozen peas
55 g (2 oz) frozen sweetcorn
340 g (12 oz) fresh beansprouts
3 tbsp soya sauce, or to taste
1 level tbsp cornflour
140 ml (¼ pt) pineapple juice without added sugar
285 g (10 oz) cooked chopped chicken

TO SERVE
a few salted peanuts (optional)

1. Put the mushrooms and onion with the garlic into a 2.3 l (4 pt) mixing bowl or very large casserole.
2. Cover and microwave on 100%/HIGH for 3 minutes.
3. Stir in the cabbage, carrot, peas, sweetcorn and the bean-sprouts.
4. Blend the cornflour with the soya sauce and a little of the pineapple juice. Stir in remaining pineapple juice.
5. Stir this liquid into the vegetables.
6. Cover and microwave on 100%/HIGH for 10 minutes. Stir twice during cooking.
7. Stir in the cooked chicken. Cover and microwave on 100%/HIGH for 1–2 minutes.
8. Allow to stand for 2 minutes, then serve sprinkled with the peanuts.

ORANGE BLANCMANGE WITH COINTREAU

Blancmange as we know it today was first served in Elizabethan England, and was improved during the reign of Queen Victoria. Unfortunately modern-day blancmange is often badly flavoured and badly made. This delicious recipe is very easy to make in the microwave and the resulting dessert is light and creamy.

PREPARATION TIME: 10 minutes
MICROWAVE COOKING TIME: 5 minutes
SERVES: 4

thinly peeled rind of 1 orange
285 ml (½ pt) semi-skimmed milk
1 dstsp castor sugar
2 tbsp clear honey
11 g (0.4 oz) sachet powdered gelatine

285 ml (½ pt) reduced-fat single cream
1 tbsp Cointreau
a little orange food-colouring

TO SERVE
slices of fresh orange

1. Put the orange rind and milk into a medium-sized mixing bowl.
2. Microwave on 100%/HIGH for 3 minutes. Stir. Set aside for 20 minutes to infuse, then strain the milk through a sieve. Stir in sugar and honey.
3. Transfer 3 tbsp of the milk to a cereal bowl. Sprinkle over the gelatine and leave to soak for 5 minutes. Then microwave the soaked gelatine for 2 minutes on 40%/SIMMER. Stir to ensure gelatine has dissolved.
4. Add the dissolved gelatine to remaining milk, stirring well.
5. Stir in the single cream with the Cointreau and the orange food-colouring. Continue to stir frequently until mixture is cold.
6. Pour into a wetted 565 ml (1 pt) mould and refrigerate until set firm.
7. Turn out and serve with slices of fresh orange.

ASPARAGUS-STUFFED CHICKEN BREASTS

What a pity that asparagus is not as readily available now as it used to be. Due to our short season and the price of fresh asparagus I have used a can of asparagus pieces in this recipe. The flavour is delicious and the pieces of chicken look most attractive on a dinner-party table with a garnish of fresh watercress. Serve with a cheese sauce.

PREPARATION TIME: 25 minutes
MICROWAVE COOKING TIME: 12–15 minutes
SERVES: 4

4 skinned and boned chicken breasts, each weighing about 170g (6 oz)
1 medium onion, chopped
30 g (1 oz) fresh brown breadcrumbs
411 g (14½ oz) can asparagus cuts and tips, drained
grated rind of ½ orange
salt and freshly ground black pepper
30 g (1 oz) herb-and-garlic butter, melted

TO GARNISH
asparagus spears
fresh watercress

1. Lay the chicken breasts one at a time between two sheets of dampened greaseproof paper and roll with a rolling pin to flatten.
2. Put the onion into a medium-sized mixing bowl and microwave, covered, on 100%/HIGH for 2 minutes. Stir in the breadcrumbs.
3. Set aside a few of the best heads of drained asparagus pieces for garnish and chop the remainder.
4. Add chopped asparagus to the onion and breadcrumbs with the orange rind and seasoning. Mix well.
5. Divide the stuffing evenly between the four chicken breasts spreading it all over but not quite to the edge.
6. Roll up each prepared breast and lift them into a shallow round dish. Secure with wooden cocktail sticks if it seems as though they might unroll.
7. Brush all over with the melted herb-and-garlic butter.
8. Cover and microwave on 70%/ROAST for 10–13 minutes.
9. Allow to stand for 5 minutes, then garnish with asparagus spears and fresh watercress and serve with a coating cheese sauce.

Rhubarb Cheese

This delicious combination of stewed rhubarb with medium-fat soft cheese and whipping cream is very light. It is high in fibre and popular with children. Serve in sundae dishes with digestive biscuits or chocolate fingers.

PREPARATION TIME: 10 minutes
MICROWAVE COOKING TIME: 12–14 minutes
SERVES: 6

680 g (1½ lb) fresh rhubarb, cut into pieces
3 tbsp pure orange juice
grated rind of 1 lemon
about 6 tbsp granulated sweetener or sugar to taste
285 ml (½ pt) reduced-fat double cream, whipped
170 g (6 oz) medium-fat soft cheese
a little pink food-colouring

TO GARNISH
sprigs of fresh mint

1. Put the rhubarb into a large bowl. Add the orange juice.
2. Cover and microwave on 100%/HIGH for about 12–14 minutes, or until the rhubarb is completely cooked. Stir 3 times. Allow to stand for 15 minutes, uncovered, then stir in lemon rind and sweetener or sugar. Allow to cool.
3. In a large mixing bowl, beat the whipped cream into the soft cheese.
4. Gradually blend the cooked rhubarb into the cheese and cream mixture. Fold in a little pink food-colouring until a pretty pink colour results.
5. Turn into wine glasses and refrigerate for 1 hour before serving.
6. Serve decorated with a sprig of mint.

BEEF ROLLS

Beef olives first appeared in British cookery in the Middle Ages. They were served as a delicacy and were sometimes made with escalopes of veal. Today they are as delicious as they ever were. They microwave extremely well and could be served with a mushroom sauce for a dinner-party main course. These are cooked quickly in a browning dish.

PREPARATION TIME: 15 minutes
MICROWAVE COOKING TIME: 7½–9½ minutes plus pre-heating time
SERVES: 4

4 thin beef frying steaks
115 g (4 oz) fresh brown breadcrumbs
1 tsp dried thyme
1 small onion, finely chopped
115 g (4 oz) button mushrooms, finely chopped
1 egg, beaten
salt and freshly ground black pepper
2 tbsp corn oil

1. Beat the steaks out with a steak hammer or with the back of a heavy knife until flat. Cut each piece in two lengthwise.
2. Make the stuffing. Put the breadcrumbs, thyme, chopped onion and mushrooms into a mixing bowl.
3. Mix well, then add the beaten egg with a little seasoning. Mix again.
4. Spread a spoonful of the stuffing on to each piece of beef.
5. Roll up and secure with string.
6. Meanwhile heat a large browning dish without its lid on 100%/HIGH for 7 minutes. Put the oil into the dish and microwave on 100%/HIGH for 1½ minutes.
7. Put the beef olives into the dish, pressing and then turning each one over so that each side is pressed on to the hot dish.
8. Microwave on 100%/HIGH for 6–8 minutes. Allow to stand for 5 minutes, then serve with a mushroom sauce.

SPICY MEATBALLS

These little meatballs are best made small (about the size of small walnuts) and served on cocktail sticks with the minty mayonnaise sauce in a separate bowl (see p. 174). Guests are invited to dip their meatballs in the sauce before eating them. They also make a substantial family meal if rolled a little larger and served with vegetables and a hot tomato or curry sauce.

PREPARATION TIME: 12 minutes
MICROWAVE COOKING TIME: 9–10 minutes
MAKES: about 21 meatballs

2.5 cm (1″) piece root ginger, peeled and finely chopped
170 g (6 oz) lean minced beef
225 g (8 oz) pork sausage-meat
1 clove garlic, crushed
55 g (2 oz) fresh brown breadcrumbs
1 tbsp freshly chopped parsley
1 tsp hot curry powder
1 tbsp soya sauce

1. In a mixing bowl combine the ginger, beef, sausage-meat, garlic, breadcrumbs, parsley, curry powder and soya sauce. Mix well with the hands.
2. Using damp hands, roll the meat mixture into small balls.
3. Arrange in a ring on a microwave roasting rack or on 4 sheets of absorbent kitchen paper arranged on a dinner plate.
4. Microwave on 70%/ROAST for 9–10 minutes.
5. Serve warm or cold after a standing time of 4 minutes.

MINTY MAYONNAISE SAUCE

A lightly flavoured minty mayonnaise is delicious served as a dip with the meatballs on p. 173. This is so easy to make using the metal blade on a food processor.

PREPARATION TIME: 5 minutes
MICROWAVE COOKING TIME: Nil

1 egg yolk
1 egg, size 3
285 ml (½ pt) olive oil
salt and freshly ground black pepper
3 sprigs fresh mint, finely chopped
2 tsp lemon juice
1 tbsp tarragon or white wine vinegar

1. Put the egg yolk and the egg into a food processor with a metal blade, or a liquidizer. Process for a few seconds.
2. With the machine running, add the oil a drop at a time to start with, then more quickly as the mayonnaise thickens.
3. Season and add the chopped mint, lemon juice and vinegar.
4. Pour into serving dish and chill until ready to serve.

STEAK AND KIDNEY PUDDING

This healthier version of steak and kidney pud uses only a lid of suet-crust pastry, which is added once the meat is tender. A different way of cooking this traditional dish, which, in olden times, often had oysters cooked with the meat. Serve with boiled new potatoes and peas.

PREPARATION TIME: 20 minutes
MICROWAVE COOKING TIME: 1 hour 13 minutes
SERVES: 4

450 g (1 lb) braising steak
115 g (4 oz) ox kidney
1 medium onion, chopped

1 beef stock cube, crumbled
1 rounded tbsp flour
1 tbsp tomato purée
115 g (4 oz) button mushrooms
170 g (6 oz) suet-crust pastry made using self-raising wholemeal flour and vegetable suet

1. Put the steak and kidney into a casserole dish with the onion and the crumbled stock cube. Sprinkle over the flour, then toss the meat in it.
2. Add the tomato purée. Pour over 115 ml (4 fl oz) water. Stir.
3. Cover with a lid and microwave on 100%/HIGH for 8 minutes. Stir well.
4. Cover and microwave on 40%/SIMMER for 1 hour, stirring and re-covering 3 times during cooking.
5. Stir in the mushrooms and set aside, covered, for 15 minutes.
6. Turn the cooked steak and kidney with its liquid into a boil-proof 565 ml (1 pt) pudding basin.
7. Roll out the pastry to fit the top of the dish.
8. Moisten rim of dish and arrange pastry on top of meat. Cover with polyethylene clingfilm, pierced 2 or 3 times.
9. Microwave on 70%/ROAST for 5 minutes.
10. Allow to stand for 5 minutes, then serve immediately.

WHOLEFOOD CHRISTMAS PUDDING

This Christmas pudding is made with wholemeal flour and dried fruits. No sugar is needed due to the sweetness of the fruit. The orange juice makes the pudding nice and moist. The pudding can be cooked in advance and stored, but must be eaten within one month.

PREPARATION TIME: 20 minutes
MICROWAVE COOKING TIME: 12 minutes for each pudding
SERVES: makes 2 puds; each will serve 6

170 g (6 oz) plain wholemeal flour
140 g (5 oz) brown breadcrumbs
115 g (4 oz) vegetable suet
1 tsp allspice
1 small eating apple, peeled and grated
1 medium carrot, peeled and grated
30 g (1 oz) dried apricots, chopped
85 g (3 oz) walnuts, finely chopped
225 g (8 oz) stoned raisins
115 g (4 oz) stoned dates
225 g (8 oz) sultanas
grated rind and juice of 2 oranges
2 tbsp black treacle
3 eggs, size 2
285 ml (10 fl oz) semi-skimmed milk
2 tbsp brandy (optional)

1. Put the flour and breadcrumbs into a large mixing bowl. Mix in the vegetable suet.
2. Add the spice, the apple, the carrot, the dried apricots, the walnuts, raisins, dates and sultanas. Mix well.
3. In a small bowl mix together the rind and juice from the oranges with the black treacle. In another bowl beat together the eggs and milk. Add brandy, if using.
4. Stir these liquid ingredients into the dry ingredients, mixing until well combined.
5. Divide the mixture between 2 × 850 ml (1½ pt) boil-proof plastic pudding basins. Cover with polyethylene clingfilm and pierce.
6. Microwave each pudding separately on 70%/ROAST for 12 minutes, giving the dish half a turn twice during cooking. Remove from microwave and allow to stand, covered, for 15 minutes, before turning out.

NOTE: To re-heat the pudding after storage: stand pudding on a plate and cover with an upturned pudding basin. Microwave on 70%/ROAST for 4–5 minutes. Allow to stand for 4 minutes before serving.

A slice of pudding may be re-heated, uncovered, on a plate for 30–45 seconds on 70%/ROAST.

SUMMER PUDDING

This attractive pudding is full of fibre and very filling. I like to have a jug of half-cream, which is fairly low in calories, to serve with the pud. A delicious summer dessert. The fruit can be varied, as any of the summer fruits will do.

PREPARATION TIME: 20 minutes
MICROWAVE COOKING TIME: 5–7 minutes
SERVES: 6

900 g (2 lb) mixed soft fruits, e.g. strawberries, raspberries, loganberries, blackcurrants, redcurrants
2 tbsp clear honey, or to taste
8 slices brown bread from a large cut loaf, 1 day old, with crusts removed

1. Put the fruit and honey into a large mixing bowl.
2. Cover and microwave on 100%/HIGH for 5–7 minutes, or until the juices begin to run from the fruit.
3. Line the base and sides of an 825 ml (1½ pt) pudding basin with enough slices of bread to cover it, reserving some to use as a lid.
4. Reserve about 3 tbsp of fruit juice. Spoon the fruit and the rest of the juice into the bread-lined bowl.
5. Use remaining bread to form a lid on top of the fruit.
6. Choose a saucer that fits inside the pudding basin and put this over the bread.
7. Put a heavy weight on top of the saucer and refrigerate the pudding overnight.
8. Turn pudding very carefully on to a serving dish and serve with the reserved juice. Hand a jug of cream round separately.

VEAL, PORK AND SPINACH LOAF

Meat loaves have been popular since medieval times, when minced pork or chicken was mixed with breadcrumbs and onions and served to workmen. Today many different recipes are available. Select lean meats for this colourful meat loaf, which is delicious served hot with vegetables or cold in slices for a buffet table.

PREPARATION TIME: 20 minutes
MICROWAVE COOKING TIME: 20 minutes
SERVES: 6

225 g (8 oz) packet frozen chopped spinach leaf
450 g (1 lb) stewing veal or minced lamb
225 g (8 oz) pork fillet
225 g (8 oz) pork sausage-meat
1 clove garlic, crushed
55 g (2 oz) fresh brown breadcrumbs
1 small onion, finely chopped
1 tsp dried mixed herbs
salt and freshly ground black pepper
1 egg, size 2

TO GARNISH
sprigs of fresh watercress

1. Split the spinach packet open with a knife.
2. Lay the packet flat on a plate and microwave on 100%/HIGH for 3–4 minutes, or until thawed.
3. Turn the spinach into a sieve and press out excess moisture.
4. Use the metal blade on a food processor. Put the veal or lamb and the pork fillet into the food processor. Chop finely.
5. Put the sausage-meat, garlic, breadcrumbs and onion into a large bowl. Add the processed meats and the herbs.
6. Season with salt and pepper and add the spinach.
7. Beat the egg lightly and add. Using the hands mix the ingredients together.
8. Press into a 1 kg (2 lb) microwave loaf pan. Level the surface.

9. Cover and microwave on 70%/ROAST for 20 minutes. Turn the dish half a turn twice during this time.
10. Allow to stand for 10 minutes. Pour off any excess fat.
11. Turn meat loaf out and serve hot or cold.

LAMB COBBLER

A spicy lamb stew served with a scone topping, which is sprinkled with grated parmesan. This one-pot meal is best served as soon as the scones are cooked, but, if preferred, the meat may be cooked earlier in the day and re-heated before adding the scone dough.

PREPARATION TIME: 15 minutes
MICROWAVE COOKING TIME: 36 minutes
SERVES: 4

1 onion, chopped
2 sticks celery, chopped
1 tsp dried dill weed
1 level tbsp mild curry powder
1 level tbsp plain flour
140 ml (¼ pt) chicken stock, warm
2 tbsp orange marmalade
1 eating apple, peeled, cored and chopped
680 g (1½ lb) boneless lean lamb, minced

FOR THE SCONE TOPPING
225 g (8 oz) self-raising flour } sieved
½ tsp baking powder } together
55 g (2 oz) margarine
½ tsp dried parsley
1 egg, size 3, beaten with 5 tbsp milk

TO SERVE
grated Parmesan (optional)

1. Put the onion and celery into a large casserole. Cover and microwave on 100%/HIGH for 3 minutes. Stir in the dill weed, curry powder and flour.

2. Gradually stir in the stock. Add the marmalade and the eating apple with the minced lamb. Stir well.
3. Cover and microwave on 100%/HIGH for 7 minutes. Stir.
4. Continue to microwave, covered, on 40%/SIMMER for 20 minutes. Stir once halfway through.
5. Meanwhile prepare the scone topping. Put the flour and baking powder into a 1.7 l (3 pt) mixing bowl. Rub in the margarine. Add the parsley, beaten egg and milk and mix to a soft dough.
6. Knead lightly, and quickly roll out to a thickness of 1 cm (½″). Using a 2.5 cm (1″) pastry-cutter, cut dough into scones.
7. Arrange the scones on top of the lamb. Cook, uncovered, on 100%/HIGH for 6 minutes.
8. Allow to stand for 5 minutes, then serve sprinkled with the grated Parmesan, if using.
9. Brown under a pre-heated grill before serving, as long as a grill-proof dish has been used.

CREAM CARAMEL

This creamy dessert tastes so different from custard made with custard powder. Serve it with fresh raspberries or strawberries, when in season, or some stewed Bramley's apples.

PREPARATION TIME: 10 minutes
MICROWAVE COOKING TIME: 20 minutes
SERVES: 4

FOR THE CARAMEL
3 tbsp castor sugar
3 tbsp water

FOR THE CUSTARD
285 ml (½ pt) milk
3 eggs, size 3, beaten
1–2 tbsp granulated sweetener, to taste
2 tsp vanilla essence

1. Make the caramel. Put the sugar and water into a Pyrex jug. Microwave on 100%/HIGH for 5–6 minutes, or until caramelized. Do not cover or stir.
2. Pour caramel into 850 ml (1½ pt) wetted dish.
3. Put the milk into a clean jug and microwave on 100%/HIGH for 2 minutes. Slowly pour heated milk on to beaten eggs, beating continuously. Add granulated sweetener and vanilla. Mix well.
4. Pour egg mixture carefully on to caramel.
5. Microwave, uncovered, on 40%/SIMMER for about 12 minutes.
6. Cool until set, then turn out on to serving dish and serve with fruit in season.

DESSERTS

During the sixteenth century, desserts started to be served as a separate course. Before this period a selection of dishes, both sweet and savoury, were placed on the table, and people ate whatever took their fancy in any combination of sweet and savoury.

Pies filled with cooked fruit and fruits in syrup were popular from the fifteenth century onwards, and from Tudor times, milk and cream were more often used for a variety of sweet dishes such as blancmanges, trifles, junkets and syllabubs.

The recipes in the dessert section of this book give a healthy slant to traditional puddings. Very few pastry dishes are given and dried fruit supplements or replaces sugar where possible. Fruit is used widely for its high-fibre, low-fat content. Try the recipes and see just how easy it is to include in a meal a healthy but delicious dessert, which, when cooked in the microwave, saves time and washing-up.

RASPBERRY AND BANANA WHIP

A light refreshing dessert, which may be made from fresh or frozen raspberries. Use low-fat yoghurt and decorate the desserts with reserved fresh raspberries, if available. A little grated chocolate is an excellent decoration when fresh fruit is unavailable.

PREPARATION TIME: 15 minutes
MICROWAVE COOKING TIME: 1–2 minutes
SERVES: 4

225 g (8 oz) raspberries fresh or frozen, de-frosted if frozen
140 ml (5 fl oz) low-fat strawberry yoghurt
2 tbsp skimmed milk
½ a tablet of strawberry jelly
2 egg whites, size 3
1 large ripe banana

TO SERVE
a few fresh raspberries or a little grated chocolate

1. Reserve 8 raspberries for decoration and put remainder into food processor or liquidizer. Add yoghurt and skimmed milk and process until smooth.
2. Put the jelly, broken into cubes, into a medium-sized jug or bowl. Add 2 tbsp water.
3. Microwave, uncovered, on 100%/HIGH for 1–2 minutes. Stir to ensure jelly has melted.
4. Pour into food processor or liquidizer and process just to combine. Sieve into large mixing bowl.
5. Whip egg whites until stiff and fold into mixture.
6. Slice banana and divide between 4 serving glasses.
7. Spoon mixture over banana slices. Chill until ready to serve.
8. Serve decorated with fresh raspberries or a little grated chocolate.

Flummeries, fruit fools, and moulds made from flavoured milk set with gelatine were all very popular in Elizabethan England. I have devised this raspberry whip to be of similar texture to a fool, but it uses healthy, low-sugar and low-fat ingredients.

MOCHA MOULDS

Sadly egg custard has for many years been associated with cookery for invalids. Try this slightly more substantial coffee version, which is served with a single swirl of whipping cream and a little grated chocolate – good enough to grace any dinner-party table.

PREPARATION TIME: 10 minutes
MICROWAVE COOKING TIME: 23 minutes
SERVES: 6

565 ml (1 pt) milk
4 eggs, size 2, lightly beaten
1 tsp instant coffee granules, dissolved in a tiny amount of hot water
½ tsp ground allspice
30 g (1 oz) soft brown sugar

TO SERVE
85 ml (3 fl oz) reduced-fat double cream, whipped
grated chocolate

1. Beat together the milk and eggs in a large mixing bowl. Add dissolved coffee and allspice. Stir well.
2. Strain mixture into 6 individual serving dishes (ramekins are ideal). The straining is easy if you use a tea-strainer, which must be spotlessly clean.
3. Divide sugar between dishes.
4. Microwave, uncovered, on 50%/MEDIUM for about 23 minutes, or until set, giving the dishes half a turn 2 or 3 times during cooking.
5. Allow to stand until cold, then chill until ready to serve.
6. Pipe a rosette of whipped cream on each mould before serving, and decorate with a little grated chocolate.

APPLE FLAN

This recipe adapts a traditional pastry recipe with a fruit filling, making it lighter and therefore lower in calories. Toasted flaked almonds are sprinkled over the dessert just before serving.

It still seems amazing to me that I am able to cook the prepared pastry flan case in the microwave in the time it takes to prepare coffee for myself and a friend!

PREPARATION TIME: 20 minutes
MICROWAVE COOKING TIME: 11–14 minutes
SERVES: 4

FOR THE PASTRY
85 g (3 oz) polyunsaturated margarine, cold from fridge
170 g (6 oz) plain flour, sieved

FOR THE FILLING
450 g (1 lb) Bramley's apples, cored, peeled and sliced
rind of ½ lemon
½ tsp lemon juice
30 g (1 oz) soft brown sugar
1 tbsp redcurrant jelly

TO SERVE
55 g (2 oz) flaked almonds, toasted (see p.49)

1. To make the pastry, put the margarine into a medium-sized mixing bowl and microwave on 100%/HIGH for 10 seconds just to soften it.
2. Add 2 tbsp water and one-third of the flour to the bowl and mix with a fork to combine. Add remaining flour and continue to mix until a dough is formed.
3. Knead lightly and roll out. Use to line an 18 cm (7") flan dish.
4. Prick sides and base with a fork and line with a sheet of absorbent kitchen paper. Refrigerate for 20 minutes.
5. Meanwhile prepare the filling. Put the apples, lemon rind and juice and the sugar into a medium-sized bowl or casserole. Cover and microwave on 100%/HIGH for 6–7 minutes, stirring after 3 minutes. Stand for 5 minutes.
6. Beat to a purée and set aside to cool.
7. Microwave the flan for 3 minutes on 100%/HIGH, then remove the paper and continue to microwave on 100%/HIGH for 1–2 minutes, or until the pastry is dry.
8. Put the redcurrant jelly into a cup and microwave on 40%/SIMMER until melted (1–2 minutes).
9. Using a pastry brush, brush the base and sides all over with the redcurrant jelly.
10. Pour the apple filling into the flan case and top with the toasted almonds.
11. Serve immediately with reduced-fat single cream or low-fat natural yoghurt.

In Elizabethan England, sweet pies and flans were often filled with a mixture of apple purées and spices. Later, fruit was mixed with candied peel. Today apple tart or pie still figures largely in the popularity stakes of many British people.

LIGHT RHUBARB CHEESECAKE

Cheesecake was traditionally a mixture of eggs, milk and curd, cream or cottage cheese, baked with the addition of raisins or currants in a pastry case and then served cold. In recent years many different recipes for uncooked cheesecakes have evolved. This one uses rhubarb yoghurt, lemon juice and sieved cottage cheese set with gelatine to produce a light cheesecake. The lemon and rhubarb topping complements the crisp ginger base well.

PREPARATION TIME: 15 minutes
MICROWAVE COOKING TIME: 3½ minutes
SERVES: 6

45 g (1½ oz) low-fat spread
170 g (6 oz) ginger or wholewheat digestive biscuits, crushed

FOR THE FILLING
11 g (0.4 oz) sachet powdered gelatine
225 g (8 oz) cottage cheese, sieved
3 × 125 g (4½ oz) cartons low-fat rhubarb yoghurt
grated rind of 1 lemon
2 tsp lemon juice
2 tsp castor sugar

TO DECORATE
115 g (4 oz) green grapes or a few fresh strawberries

1. Sprinkle the gelatine over 2 tbsp cold water in a soup or cereal bowl and set aside for 10–15 minutes.
2. Put the low-fat spread into a bowl and microwave on 40%/SIMMER for 1½–2 minutes, or until melted.
3. Stir in the crushed biscuits. (The best way to crush them is to break them into pieces, put the pieces into a food processor and process them briefly.)
4. Stir the biscuit crumbs into the melted margarine, then press the mixture over the base of a loose-bottomed 200 cm (8″) cake tin. Refrigerate to set firm.
5. Combine the sieved cottage cheese with the rhubarb yoghurt and the rind and juice of the lemon. Mix well.

6. Microwave the gelatine for 2 minutes on 40%/SIMMER. Stir to ensure gelatine has dissolved.
7. Fold the dissolved gelatine into the yoghurt and cottage cheese mixture with the castor sugar.
8. Pour on to biscuit-crumb base and refrigerate until set.
9. Carefully remove the cheesecake by pushing up the base of the tin. Set the cheesecake on a pretty serving plate and decorate with the halved grapes (remove the pips) or fresh strawberry halves before serving.

NOTE: If a food processor is available, there is no need to sieve the cottage cheese. Simply put it into the processor, using the metal blade, and process for a few seconds, then add the yoghurt and lemon rind and juice and continue to process until smooth. Add the dissolved gelatine with the castor sugar and process to combine, then continue as given.

Dried Date and Apricot Bread-and-Butter Pudding

Traditional bread-and-butter pud is an example of a dessert that has always been fairly healthy. This recipe uses dried fruit instead of sugar, and milk with low-fat spread instead of butter to make it even healthier than the original.

PREPARATION TIME: 15 minutes
MICROWAVE COOKING TIME: 19–24 minutes
SERVES: 4–6

5 slices cut from a fresh white loaf, crusts removed
low-fat spread
55 g (2 oz) dried apricots, chopped
55 g (2 oz) dates, chopped
1 Cox's apple, unpeeled, but cored and chopped
1 tsp mixed spice
425 ml (¾ pt) semi-skimmed milk
3 eggs, size 4
1 tbsp demerara sugar

1. Very lightly spread the bread on one side with the low-fat spread.
2. Sprinkle a 1.1–1.7 l (2–3 pt) fairly shallow dish, about 23 cm (9″) in diameter, with a few of the dried apricots and dates and some chopped apple.
3. Cut each slice of bread into 4 and layer into the pie dish with the rest of the fruit and the spices. Top with a final layer of bread, buttered side up.
4. Meanwhile put the milk into a large jug and microwave on 100%/HIGH for 4 minutes.
5. Beat the eggs together in a large mixing bowl and then slowly pour the heated milk on to the eggs, beating continuously.
6. Hold a sieve over the pie dish and pour the egg mixture through it on to the bread.
7. Sprinkle the demerara sugar over the surface.
8. Cover and microwave on 50%/MEDIUM for 15–20 minutes, or until custard is set.
9. Allow to stand for 5 minutes, then flash under a grill to crisp the surface if desired, and serve with natural yoghurt. This dessert is also delicious served cold with reduced-fat single cream or ice cream.

NOTE: If you wish to flash this under a grill after microwaving, remember to use a pottery or Pyrex dish that is grill-proof. However, having forgotten this important point myself, I found that, after the standing time, I could carefully turn the pudding out on to a dinner plate and then invert it on to a similar dinner plate, which was grill-proof. I served it from the dinner plate!

ORANGE JELLY WITH FRUIT

An attractive fruity jelly made from pure orange juice and gelatine. The tangy mandarin oranges and crunchy apple contrast well. Leave the skin on the apple to provide interest and fibre. Serve with low-fat orange yoghurt.

PREPARATION TIME: 15 minutes
MICROWAVE COOKING TIME: 3–4 minutes
SERVES: 6

680 ml (24 fl oz) unsweetened pure orange juice
2 × 11 g (0.4 oz) sachets powdered gelatine
1 red-skinned English eating apple, cored and chopped
298 g (10½ oz) can mandarin orange segments in natural juice, drained, reserving juice
grated rind of 1 orange

1. Put 6 tbsp pure orange juice into a small bowl. Sprinkle over the gelatine and set aside for 10 minutes.
2. Rinse an attractive 1.1 l (2 pt) jelly mould with cold water.
3. Put the prepared apples and the drained orange segments into the jelly mould.
4. Combine the juice from the mandarins with the pure orange juice.
5. Microwave the soaked gelatine, uncovered, for 3–4 minutes on 40%/SIMMER, stirring after 2 minutes. Stir to ensure gelatine has dissolved.
6. Stir dissolved gelatine into orange juice.
7. Pour the liquid jelly over the fruit.
8. Chill until set.

It is rather sad that with the availability of the modern jelly tablet, to which one simply adds boiling water to make a jelly, the cook rarely uses gelatine and fruit juice. However, it is so easy to dissolve gelatine using the microwave, and the flavour of this recipe is so good, that I hope many will be inspired to try it.

PLUM PUDDING

This traditional baked British pudding uses canned red plums for the filling and an almond-flavour sponge made with low-fat spread for the topping. It is quick to make and extremely good on a cold winter's evening. Serve with the custard sauce on page 196, or make a light sauce from the juice of the plums, thickened with arrowroot.

PREPARATION TIME: 10 minutes
MICROWAVE COOKING TIME: 5–7 minutes
SERVES: 4

567 g (1 lb 4 oz) can red plums, drained
1 tbsp medium sherry

FOR THE SPONGE
55 g (2 oz) self-raising wholemeal flour, sieved
55 g (2 oz) self-raising flour, sieved
a few drops almond essence
115 g (4 oz) low-fat dairy spread
55 g (2 oz) soft light brown sugar
2 eggs, size 2, beaten
2 tbsp milk

TO SERVE
a little sifted icing sugar

1. Put the drained plums into the base of an 850 ml (1½ pt) straight-sided soufflé dish. Add the sherry.
2. Put all the ingredients for the sponge into a mixing bowl and mix to combine, then beat with a wooden spoon for 1 minute.
3. Spread the sponge mixture evenly over the plums.
4. Microwave on 100%/HIGH 5–7 minutes, or until sponge is well risen and just set. Insert a wooden cocktail stick into the centre to test whether it is cooked. This should come out clean.
5. Sprinkle with the icing sugar and serve warm.

RHUBARB AND ORANGE JELLY

High-fibre rhubarb is grown in many English gardens. Strictly speaking it should be classed as a vegetable, as it is the stalk of the plant that is eaten. However, it is traditionally cooked and used as a sweet. It combines well with orange in this light dessert. Serve with ice-cream.

PREPARATION TIME: 15 minutes
MICROWAVE COOKING TIME: 9–11 minutes
SERVES: 4–6

11 g (0.4 oz) sachet + 2 level tsp powdered gelatine
225 g (8 oz) prepared rhubarb, cut into 2.5 cm (1″) pieces
2 tbsp orange marmalade
55 g (2 oz) castor sugar
rind and juice of 1 orange
285 ml (10 fl oz) Sauterne or Riesling (medium-sweet) white wine

1. Put 3 tbsp water into a soup bowl. Sprinkle over the gelatine and set aside for 10 minutes.
2. Put the prepared rhubarb into a medium-sized casserole. Add the marmalade, the castor sugar and the orange rind and juice. Cover and microwave on 100%/HIGH for 6–8 minutes, stirring and re-covering after 4 minutes. Stir and set aside for 10 minutes.
3. Put the cooked rhubarb into a food processor or liquidizer and process until smooth. Turn into a large bowl. Stir in the wine with 3 tbsp water.
4. Microwave the gelatine for 3 minutes on 40%/SIMMER. Stir to ensure gelatine has dissolved.
5. Stir dissolved gelatine into rhubarb. Pour into a wetted mould (see note) and refrigerate until set.

NOTE: Use an 850 ml (1½ pt) re-usable microwave ring mould to set the jelly in. When firm, turn out and fill the centre with drained, canned fruit or strawberries, when in season.

APRICOT CRUMBLE

The apricots in this recipe are cooked with raisins, and as the raisins are very sweet, this means that the amount of sugar in the recipe can be reduced considerably. Similarly, although I have added some desiccated coconut (which contains oil) to the crumble topping, the crumble is made from a low-fat spread, so the fat content is less than that of a traditional crumble recipe. Serve with low-fat natural yoghurt.

PREPARATION TIME: 15 minutes
MICROWAVE COOKING TIME: 10 minutes
SERVES: 4

450 g (1 lb) fresh apricots, halved and stoned
55 g (2 oz) raisins
55 g (2 oz) soft brown sugar

FOR THE CRUMBLE TOPPING

170 g (6 oz) wholemeal flour
½ tsp allspice
85 g (3 oz) low-fat dairy spread, cold from fridge
30 g (1 oz) desiccated coconut
55 g (2 oz) demerara sugar

1. Put the apricots, raisins and soft brown sugar into a 1.4 l (2½ pt) grill-proof casserole dish.
2. Put the flour and allspice into a mixing bowl. Rub in the low-fat spread until the mixture resembles fine breadcrumbs.
3. Add the coconut and demerara sugar. Mix well.
4. Sprinkle the topping evenly over the fruit.
5. Microwave, uncovered, on 100%/HIGH for about 10 minutes.
6. Allow to stand for 5 minutes, then crisp briefly under a pre-heated grill. Serve immediately.

Carob and Apricot Pudding

Carob powder is a healthier alternative to cocoa powder and is readily available in health-food shops. It is lower in calories and higher in fibre and iron. This pudding also uses high-fibre dried apricots, which combine well with the chocolatey flavour. Serve with the carob sauce or the custard sauce on page 196.

PREPARATION TIME: 10 minutes
MICROWAVE COOKING TIME: 5–7 minutes
SERVES: 4

85 g (3 oz) self-raising flour } **sieved together**
30 g (1 oz) carob powder }
55 g (2 oz) castor sugar }
55 g (2 oz) dried apricots, chopped
grated rind of 1 orange + 2 tbsp squeezed orange juice
2 large eggs, size 2
115 g (4 oz) polyunsaturated margarine

1. Very lightly grease an 850 ml (1½ pt) pudding basin.
2. Put all ingredients except the dried apricots into a mixing bowl and, using a wooden spoon, mix to combine, then continue to beat for 1 minute. Fold apricots in.
3. Transfer the mixture to the prepared pudding basin. Level the top. Cover.
4. Microwave on 100%/HIGH for 5–7 minutes, or until well risen and springy to the touch.
5. Allow to stand for 5 minutes, then turn out and serve with carob sauce.

Cocoa was brought to our shops from Jamaica as long ago as the 1650s. The first English factory for processing cocoa beans was set up in 1728, a century before chocolate bars were produced.

CAROB SAUCE

The consistency of this sauce may be varied according to how you want to use it. Sometimes I use hardly any milk and make it into a thick icing, which I use as a filling for cakes. The amount of milk given below makes it into a pouring sauce suitable for serving with puddings.

PREPARATION TIME: 5 minutes
MICROWAVE COOKING TIME: 2–3 minutes
SERVES: 5

30 g (1 oz) polyunsaturated margarine
1 rounded tbsp carob powder, sieved
115 g (4 oz) sifted icing sugar
55 ml (2 fl oz) milk

1. Put the margarine and carob powder into a medium-sized mixing bowl. Microwave on 40%/SIMMER for 2 minutes, stirring after 1 minute.
2. Stir in the sifted icing sugar with the milk, mixing to a smooth consistency. Serve cold.
3. To serve hot, microwave on 100%/HIGH for 1 minute after mixing in the sugar. Stir well and serve in a jug.

CUSTARD SAUCE

Real custard tastes considerably better than the variety we make from commercially prepared powder. Stirring the custard (see step 5) is very important, to prevent the mixture from curdling. The result should be a delicious hot sauce the consistency of cream and the colour of clotted cream.

PREPARATION TIME: 10 minutes
MICROWAVE COOKING TIME: 5–6 minutes
SERVES: 3

2 eggs, size 2
285 ml (½ pt) semi-skimmed milk
½–1 tsp vanilla essence
1 level tbsp granulated sugar
1½ level tbsp cornflour

1. Put the eggs into a 1.7 l (3 pt) mixing bowl and beat lightly using a balloon whisk.
2. Put the milk and vanilla essence into a jug and microwave on 100%/HIGH for 2 minutes.
3. Pour the heated milk slowly on to the eggs, beating continuously with the balloon whisk. Add the sugar.
4. Blend the cornflour with just enough water to produce a smooth paste and add this to the egg and milk mixture, beating again with the balloon whisk.
5. Microwave, uncovered, on 100%/HIGH for 3–4 minutes, stirring with the balloon whisk about every 40 seconds until the custard thickens.
6. Serve hot or cold.

NOTE: The flavour of the custard can be varied by omitting the vanilla essence and adding the zest of an orange or lemon, or using a little almond essence or a spoonful of brandy.

SPOTTED DICK

A wonderful nursery pudding, which cooks in the microwave in just 6 or 7 minutes. This recipe uses vegetable margarine instead of the more usual beef suet. Serve with custard sauce (page 196).

PREPARATION TIME: 10 minutes
MICROWAVE COOKING TIME: 6–7 minutes
SERVES: 6

85 g (3 oz) self-raising flour
85 g (3 oz) brown breadcrumbs
85 g (3 oz) vegetable margarine, cold from fridge
30 g (1 oz) soft brown sugar (optional)
grated rind of 1 orange
170 g (6 oz) sultanas
about 5–6 tbsp semi-skimmed milk

1. Mix together the flour and breadcrumbs. Rub in the margarine.
2. Add the sugar, orange rind and the sultanas. Mix well.
3. Make a well in the centre of the dry ingredients and stir in enough milk to give a fairly firm but not sticky dough.
4. Shape into an oblong and turn into a lightly greased re-usable 18 cm (7″) microwave ring mould.
5. Cover and microwave on 70%/ROAST for 6–7 minutes.
6. Allow to stand, covered, for 5 minutes, then turn out and serve with custard sauce.

BAKED APPLES

Mrs Beeton suggested filling the cavities of baked apples with apple parings while baking them, and then replacing these with jam when ready to serve. The high sugar content of the filling often throws the timing when microwaving baked apples, as the centre tends to cook too quickly. However, I find this method of starting the apples without a filling very successful. Serve with ice cream or low-fat natural yoghurt.

PREPARATION TIME: 10 minutes
MICROWAVE COOKING TIME: 11 minutes
SERVES: 4

4 large Bramley's apples
115 g (4 oz) marzipan
2 tbsp pure orange juice
4 dstsp clear honey

TO DECORATE
a few toasted flaked almonds (see page 49)

1. Core the apples, using an apple corer. Retain a small piece from the end of each core and use this to fit back into the bottom of each apple as a 'bung'.
2. With a small, sharp knife make a shallow cut right round each apple about 2.5 cm (1″) from the top.
3. Put the apples into a shallow dish. Pour over the orange juice. Cover and microwave on 100%/HIGH for 6 minutes.
4. Meanwhile divide marzipan into 4 even-sized pieces. Shape each piece of marzipan into a barrel and use to fill cavities, pushing in well.
5. Top each apple with a dessertspoonful of honey.
6. Re-cover apples and continue to microwave on 70% ROAST for about 4–5 minutes. Baste occasionally with the sauce.
7. Allow to stand for 10 minutes.
8. Sprinkle the toasted flaked almonds over the apples and serve.

NOTE: When removed from the microwave the apples will still look quite green, although they should give slightly when pressed. During the standing time they will lose their bright colour as they finish cooking.

CARAMELIZED ORANGE AND GRAPEFRUIT

I love the sharp contrast of grapefruit and orange slices in this traditional caramel sweet. Take care *not* to use any sort of plastic dish when making the caramel, as it does get exceptionally hot.

PREPARATION TIME: 15 minutes
MICROWAVE COOKING TIME: 11–12 minutes
SERVES: 4

3 seedless oranges, washed
1 grapefruit, washed
1 tbsp kirsch
170 g (6 oz) castor sugar

TO SERVE
natural yoghurt

TO DECORATE
a few fresh mint leaves, if available

1. Peel 1 orange very thinly, taking care not to remove any pith with the rind. Cut this peel into very thin strips and reserve. Do the same with a little of the grapefruit peel. (I find it easiest to remove the peel, initially, with a potato peeler; this way it is fairly easy to avoid removing any of the bitter pith.)
2. Peel the fruit, removing all pith and skin. Discard any pips from grapefruit. Peel the fruit over a large bowl, as when you remove the peel, some of the juice runs out, and this juice should be reserved.
3. Slice fruit thinly and arrange attractively in a shallow serving dish. Mix any reserved juice with the kirsch and pour over the fruit. Add the reserved peel.
4. Make the caramel. Put the sugar and 115 ml (4 fl oz) water into a 1.7 (3 pt) Pyrex mixing bowl and microwave on 100%/HIGH for about 11–12 minutes. Do not cover and do not stir. A golden caramel should result.
5. USE OVEN GLOVES. Pour the caramel over the orange and grapefruit.
6. Chill well before serving.

NOTE: Sugar refineries were first set up in London in the mid-sixteenth century, but it was not until it became more readily available in the eighteenth century that sweet-making, and in particular toffee-making, became so popular.

PEAR PUDDING

Instead of using animal suet this recipe uses vegetable suet, which is lighter and more easily digested. Filled with cinnamon-flavoured pears this delicious and sustaining pud is well worth sinning for!

PREPARATION TIME: 25 minutes
MICROWAVE COOKING TIME: 11–12 minutes
SERVES: 4

225 g (8 oz) self-raising flour
115 g (4 oz) vegetable suet
1 kg (2 lb) ripe Comice pears
1 tsp ground cinnamon
1 tbsp pure orange juice

1. Put the flour into a large mixing bowl. Fork in the suet.
2. Mix to a soft dough with about 140 ml (¼ pt) water.
3. Knead lightly, then roll out two-thirds of the pastry and use to line an 850 ml (1½ pt) boil-proof plastic pudding basin. Allow pastry to overhang slightly.
4. Reserve 1 pear for decorating cooked pud, then peel, core and chop remainder of pears.
5. Fill the pastry with prepared pears. Add cinnamon and pure orange juice.
6. Moisten the edges of the pastry.
7. Roll out remaining pastry to form a lid and top the pudding with this circle of pastry. Seal edges. Cut a small hole to allow steam to escape.
8. Use 3 pieces of absorbent kitchen paper torn off together and anchored under pudding basin at either end to form a tent-like, loose-fitting cover – to allow pastry to rise.
9. Microwave on 70%/ROAST for 11–12 minutes.
10. Allow to stand, covered, for 5 minutes.
11. Carefully run a round-bladed knife right round the edge of the pudding, then turn it out on to a dinner plate. Serve decorated with remaining pear, sliced and cored, but not peeled.

WINTER FRUIT SALAD

A colourful and light fruit salad is made by adding fresh fruits in season to dried fruits cooked in the microwave. There is no need to soak the dried fruits before microwaving them, but they must be allowed to stand after cooking to reconstitute them completely. Serve with reduced-fat single cream.

PREPARATION TIME: 10 minutes
MICROWAVE COOKING TIME: 10 minutes
SERVES: 4–6

115 g (4 oz) dried apricot halves
115 g (4 oz) dried prunes, no-need-to-soak-variety
85 g (3 oz) soft light brown sugar
565 ml (1 pt) boiling water
½ fresh lemon
1 cinnamon stick

TO ADD TO THE DRIED FRUITS
1 red apple, cored and diced
1 green apple, cored and diced
1 banana, sliced
1 large orange, peeled and segmented
115 g (4 oz) white seedless grapes

1. Put the dried apricots and prunes into a large mixing bowl. Add the sugar. Pour on the boiling water. Add the lemon with the cinnamon stick. Cover and microwave on 100%/HIGH for 10 minutes, stirring and re-covering after 5 minutes.
2. Set aside to cool completely (preferably overnight).
3. Remove cinnamon stick and lemon.
4. Add the prepared apples, banana, orange and grapes. Stir well and turn into a serving dish.

During the eighteenth century the British tried drying such fruits as plums, gooseberries and apricots to try to achieve something similar to the raisins, currants, sultanas, figs, dates, etc. that had been imported from the Middle East for centuries.

They were obviously successful, and now, because of the recent enthusiasm for healthy eating, a wide range of dried fruit is available in supermarkets and health-food shops nationwide.

RICE PUDDING

Creamy rice pudding is traditionally served with plenty of whipped double cream or clotted cream – naughty but nice! I serve this version, which is flavoured with a piece of cinnamon stick, with thick Greek yoghurt. As the pudding is made with milk and no butter it becomes a healthy dessert. A spoonful of low-sugar jam with each serving is delicious, or some reconstituted dried fruits (see recipe for winter fruit salad on page 202).

PREPARATION TIME: 5 minutes
MICROWAVE COOKING TIME: 37 minutes
SERVES: 3–4

55 g (2 oz) short-grain white rice
565 ml (1 pt) semi-skimmed milk
1 piece cinnamon stick
30 g (1 oz) raisins
1 tbsp castor sugar

1. Put the rice, milk and cinnamon stick into a large mixing bowl (see note). Add the raisins and castor sugar. Stir well.
2. Cover and microwave on 100%/HIGH for 7 minutes. Stir.
3. Re-cover and microwave on 70%/ROAST for 30 minutes. Stir twice during this time. Allow to stand for 10 minutes. Remove cinnamon stick and serve.

NOTE: A large mixing bowl or casserole with a capacity of about 3.4 l (6 pt) is necessary to stop the pudding boiling over during cooking.

GRAPEFRUIT MOUSSE

A light tangy mousse. The gelatine is dissolved in the microwave and the set mousse is decorated with slices of pink grapefruit and a little whipped cream.

PREPARATION TIME: 10 minutes
MICROWAVE COOKING TIME: 3–4 minutes
SERVES: 6

2 pink grapefruit
1 level tbsp powdered gelatine
3 eggs, size 2
85 g (3 oz) castor sugar
125 g (4½ oz) carton of mandarin low-fat yoghurt

TO DECORATE
140 ml (¼ pt) reduced-fat double cream, whipped

1. Using a zester, remove and keep the rind from one grapefruit. Cut one grapefruit in half and strain juice into medium-sized bowl. Sprinkle gelatine over and set aside for 10 minutes.
2. Peel remaining grapefruit, discarding all pith and peel. Carefully cut out segments, discarding all membranes so that you have grapefruit segments resembling those you would find in a tin of grapefruit. Arrange these on a plate. Cover and set aside for decoration.
3. Separate the eggs, putting the yolks in one large bowl and the whites in another. Add the sugar to the yolks and beat, using an electric mixer, until thick and creamy. Add the grapefruit rind.
4. Microwave the gelatine mixture on 40%/SIMMER for 3–4 minutes, or until melted. Stir frequently.
5. Add the dissolved gelatine to the whisked egg yolks and sugar. Continue whisking until combined. Fold in the yoghurt evenly.
6. Whisk egg whites and fold in lightly and evenly.
7. Pour mousse into serving dish and leave to set.

8. When set firm, pipe rosettes of whipped double cream round edge of dish.
9. Arrange the reserved grapefruit slices in an attractive pattern on the mousse and serve immediately.

SEMOLINA PUDDING WITH SULTANAS AND EGG

Semolina pudding, although often associated with school dinners, can be a delicious sweet, if cooked correctly. Historically it was often served to invalids because it is easily digested; savoury semolina recipes were also fairly popular. This version is particularly low in fat.

PREPARATION TIME: 5 minutes
MICROWAVE COOKING TIME: 15–18 minutes
SERVES: 4

565 ml (1 pt) semi-skimmed milk
4 level tbsp semolina
30 g (1 oz) soft brown sugar
55 g (2 oz) sultanas
1 egg, size 2, beaten

TO SERVE
grated nutmeg

1. Stir milk and semolina into a 1.7 l (3 pt) mixing bowl. Microwave, uncovered, on 100%/HIGH for 5–6 minutes, or until boiling. Stir frequently during cooking.
2. Continue to microwave, uncovered, on 40%/SIMMER for 10–12 minutes, stirring after 5 minutes.
3. Stir in the sugar and sultanas and set aside for 5 minutes. Stir again.
4. Stir in the beaten egg, then divide the semolina between 4 cereal bowls.
5. Top with a little grated nutmeg and serve immediately.

NOTE: This dessert may also be eaten cold.

GOOSEBERRY FOOL

Gooseberries are part of our heritage, and gooseberry fool is one of the most delicious of English desserts. This recipe uses proper custard instead of cream with the gooseberries, which results in a superb light fool.

PREPARATION TIME: 10 minutes
MICROWAVE COOKING TIME: 5 minutes
SERVES: 4

450 g (1 lb) green gooseberries, topped and tailed
140 g (5 oz) castor sugar
285 ml (½ pt) custard (see page 196), cooled

TO SERVE
sponge fingers

1 Put the gooseberries and sugar into a medium-sized casserole.
2. Add 1 tbsp water. Cover and microwave on 100%/HIGH for 5 minutes, stirring and re-covering after 3 minutes. Set aside until cool.
3. Put into food processor or liquidizer and process until smooth. Return to large casserole.
4. Fold in custard and turn into a large glass bowl or into individual sundae dishes.
5. Chill until ready to serve.

CABINET PUDDING

A traditional pudding of sponge cake with dried fruit and egg custard. Conventionally this pud needs to be steamed for about an hour, but in a 700W microwave the pud takes only 10 minutes! An attractive, speedy dessert, best accompanied by an apricot or custard sauce.

PREPARATION TIME: 15 minutes
MICROWAVE COOKING TIME: 8–9 minutes
SERVES: 4

rind of ½ lemon
55 g (2 oz) sultanas
55 g (2 oz) glacé cherries
2 tbsp sherry or kirsch
12 sponge fingers, cut up
85 g (3 oz) slice Victoria sandwich, filled with reduced-sugar jam, cut up (if not available, use 6 extra sponge fingers)
2 eggs, size 2
285 ml (½ pt) milk
45 g (1½ oz) castor sugar

TO DECORATE
glacé cherries and angelica

1. Put lemon rind, sultanas and cherries into a bowl. Pour over sherry. Microwave uncovered, for 1 minute on 100%/HIGH. Stir and set aside for 15 minutes.
2. Mix the pieces of sponge fingers and the chopped Victoria sandwich together. Put a layer of them into the bottom of an 18 cm (7″) dish.
3. Sprinkle over some of the fruit and sherry mixture.
4. Add another layer of sponge fingers and cake.
5. Continue to layer until all of the fruit mixture and sponge are used up. Finish with a layer of sponge.
6. Beat together the eggs, milk and sugar and pour over the sponge.
7. Leave to soak for 15 minutes.
8. Microwave, uncovered, on 100%/HIGH for 7–8 minutes. Turn the dish half a turn after 5 minutes.
9. Allow to stand for 5 minutes, then serve, decorated with the cherries and angelica and accompanied by a sweet sauce.

NOTE: This dessert may also be served cold.

BLACKCURRANT LAYER

Frozen blackcurrants, high in vitamin C and fibre, are available all the year round. This delicious cold sweet uses a healthy breakfast cereal, which can be bought in most supermarkets. It makes an up-to-date version of the traditional Charlotte, which simply meant stewed fruit topped or layered with a crisp mixture made of breadcrumbs, butter and sugar – delicious but high in calories and fat.

PREPARATION TIME: 5 minutes
MICROWAVE COOKING TIME: 7 minutes
SERVES: 4

340 g (12 oz) frozen blackcurrants
3 tbsp soft brown sugar
½ tsp ground cinnamon
1 rounded tsp arrowroot
285 ml (½ pt) reduced-fat double cream
rind of ½ lemon
170 g (6 oz) Jordan's Original Crunchy cereal

TO SERVE
a little grated chocolate

1. Put the blackcurrants and sugar into a medium-sized casserole with the cinnamon. Cover and microwave on 100%/HIGH for 6 minutes, stirring and re-covering after 3 minutes.
2. Blend the arrowroot to a smooth paste with a little water and stir into the cooked fruit. Microwave, uncovered, on 100%/HIGH for 1 minute, stirring well with a wooden spoon after 30 seconds and at end of cooking time. Set aside until cold.
3. To complete the dessert, whip cream until it stands in soft peaks, then fold the lemon rind into the cream.
4. Fill 4 sundae glasses with layers of breakfast cereal, whipped cream and cooled blackcurrants, finishing with a layer of cream.

5. Top each dessert with a little grated chocolate before serving.

APPLE AND APRICOT CHARLOTTE

A high-fibre fruity dessert, which is particularly popular during the winter months. Serve with Greek yoghurt or low-calorie ice cream instead of the more traditional custard. Butter is used in this recipe for its wonderful flavour.

PREPARATION TIME: 15 minutes
MICROWAVE COOKING TIME: 22 minutes
SERVES: 4

FOR THE TOPPING
70 g (2½ oz) butter
225 g (8 oz) fresh brown breadcrumbs
30 g (1 oz) flaked almonds
grated rind of 1 lemon
30 g (1 oz) demerara sugar
½ tsp ground ginger
½ tsp ground cinnamon

680 g (1½ lb) Bramley's apples, peeled and cored
115 g (4 oz) dried apricots, chopped
30 g (1 oz) raisins
1 tbsp apple juice concentrate

1. Prepare the topping. Put the butter into a large mixing bowl and microwave, uncovered, on 50%/MEDIUM for 1½ minutes, or until melted. Stir in the breadcrumbs and almonds, mixing really well with a fork until the butter is evenly absorbed.
2. Microwave, uncovered, on 100%/HIGH for 4 minutes. Stir well. Microwave on 100%/HIGH for 3 minutes. Stir. Microwave on 100%/HIGH for 2–3 minutes. Stir well and set aside. The breadcrumbs should now be crisp and golden.
3. Mix the lemon rind into the prepared topping with the sugar, ground ginger and cinnamon.

4. Slice the apples into a medium-sized, fairly shallow dish. Add the apricots, raisins and the apple juice concentrate. Stir to mix fruits evenly.
5. Spoon the topping over the prepared fruit, to cover completely.
6. Microwave, uncovered, on 100%/HIGH for 9–10 minutes, turning the dish ¼ turn twice during cooking.
7. Allow to stand, uncovered, for 5 minutes, then serve.

Apple Charlotte may well have originated in France, but it quickly became very popular in this country. Many of the 'traditional' recipes of a country originate from other countries, as all cooks borrow ideas and recipes from others, whether at home or abroad.

YOGHURT CHOCOLATE CUPS

Chocolate is so easy to melt in the microwave without the bother of putting it in a bowl over a pan of hot water. Remember, though, that it does tend to melt in its shape and will burn quickly without attention, so stir frequently while melting. Solid blocks of chocolate first became available in this country in the mid-nineteenth century.

PREPARATION TIME: 10 minutes
MICROWAVE COOKING TIME: 4–5 minutes
SERVES: 6

12 paper fairy-cake cases

115 g (4 oz) plain cooking chocolate, broken into pieces
140 ml (5 fl oz) Greek natural yoghurt
runny honey, to taste
2 bananas, sliced

TO SERVE
55 g (2 oz) walnuts, roughly chopped

1. Put the pieces of chocolate into a mixing bowl and microwave on 40%/SIMMER, uncovered, for 4–5 minutes, or until chocolate melts. Stir frequently and remove from microwave as soon as chocolate has melted.
2. Double the paper cases up so that you have 6 doubles. Arrange on a dinner plate.
3. Using a pastry brush, brush a thin layer of melted chocolate to coat the inside of each double paper case. Leave to harden for a few minutes.
4. Repeat with another layer of melted chocolate so that each chocolate cup is quite thickly coated. (It may be necessary to return chocolate to the microwave on 40%/SIMMER to melt it down again between coatings.) Refrigerate the chocolate cups until completely set – overnight if possible.
5. Carefully tear away the paper of each chocolate cup and discard.
6. Prepare the filling. Turn yoghurt into a mixing bowl. Blend in the honey.
7. Divide bananas evenly between the chocolate cups. Top with the yoghurt and honey mixture.
8. Sprinkle each chocolate cup with some of the chopped walnuts before serving.

INDEX